SKULL COLORING BOOK

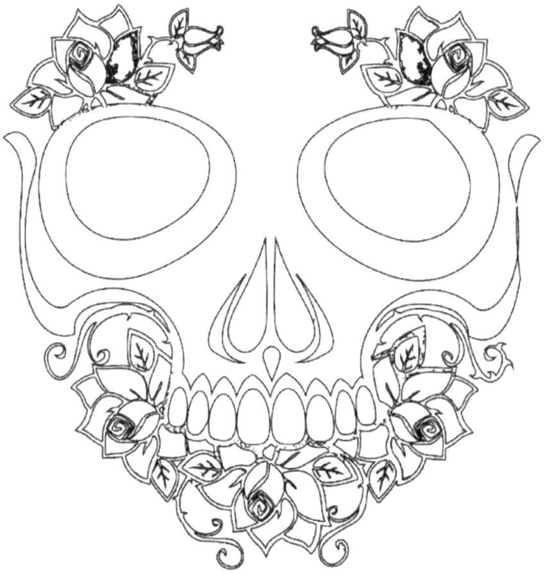

ISBN: 9781728909257

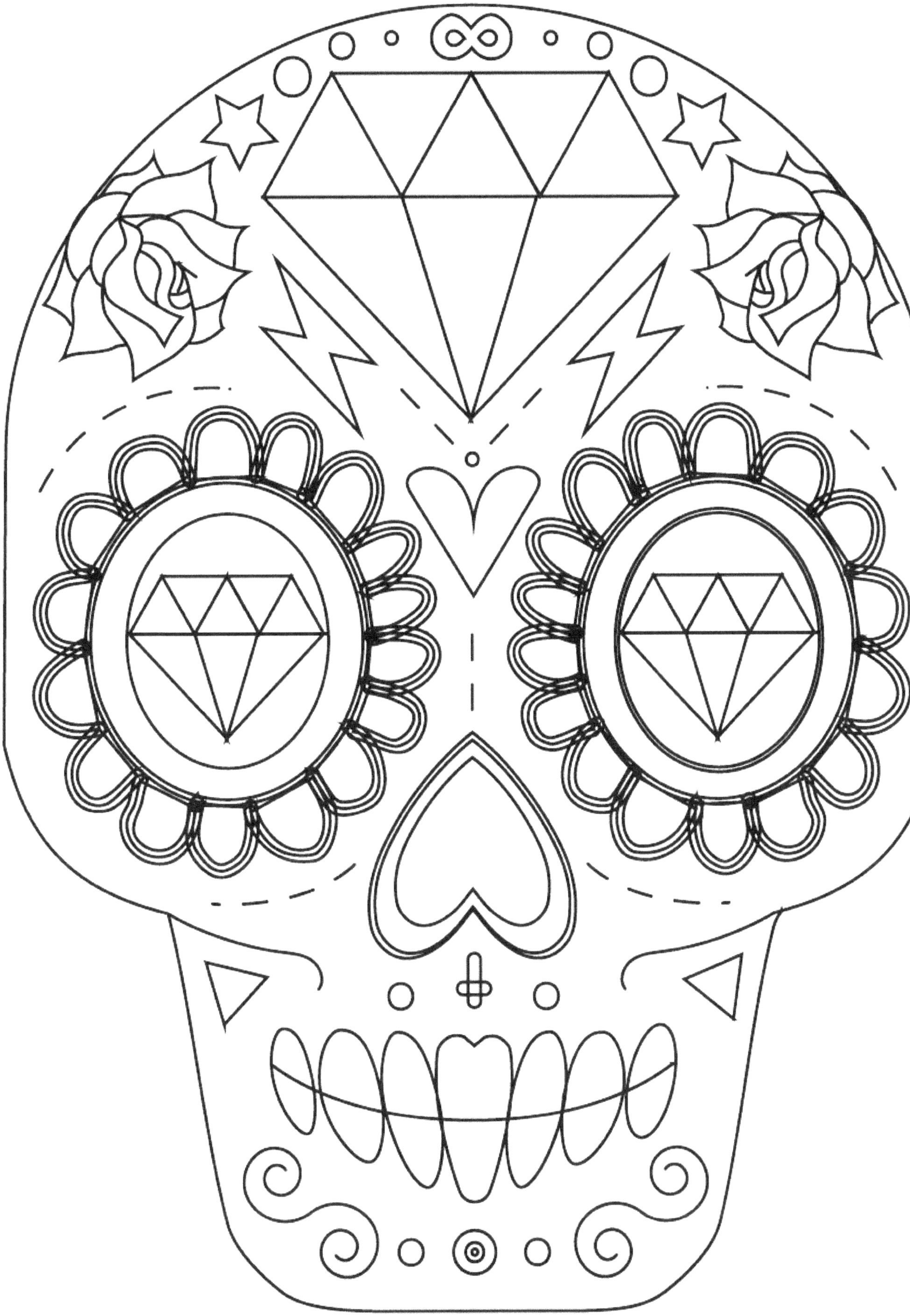

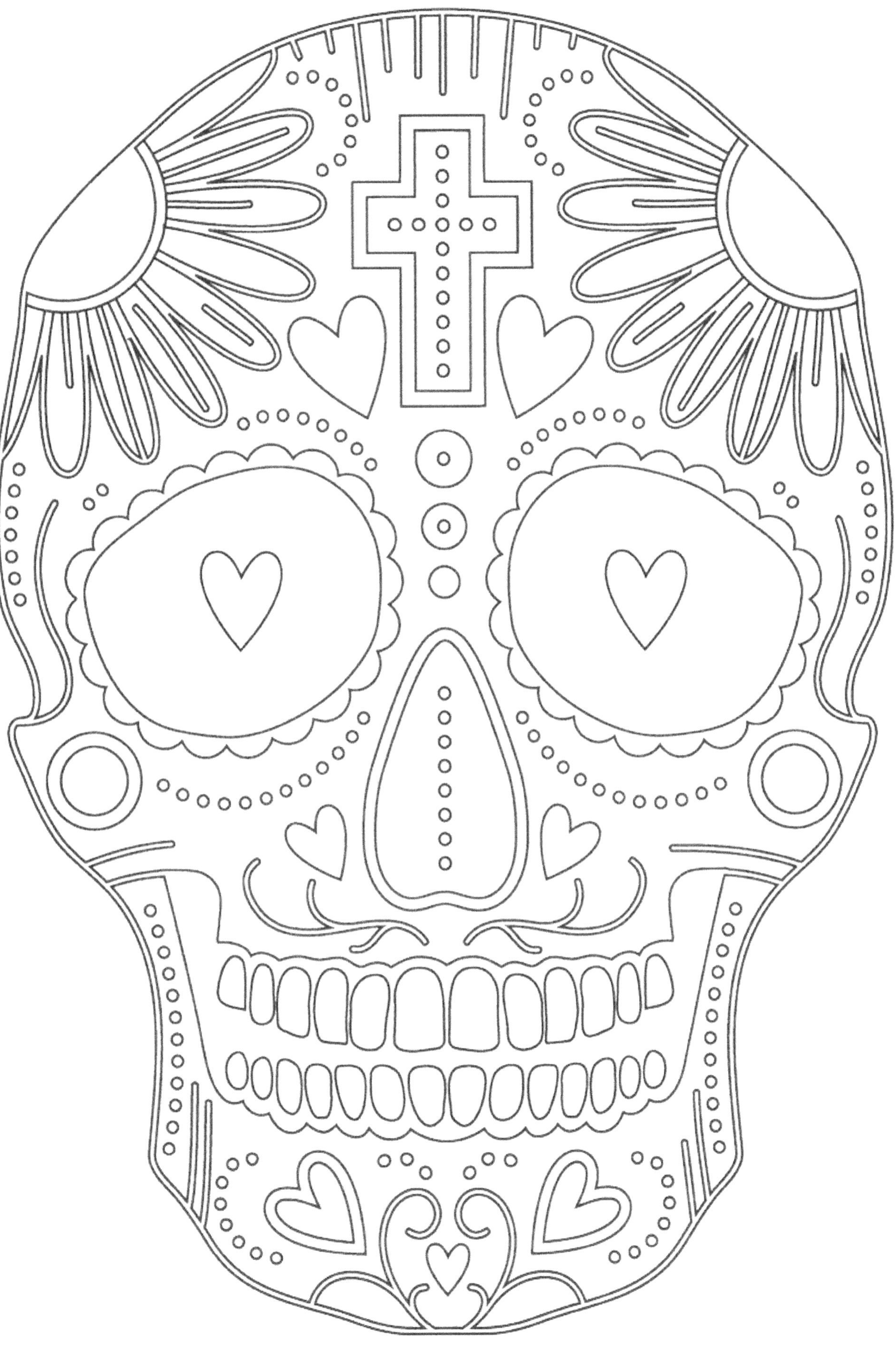

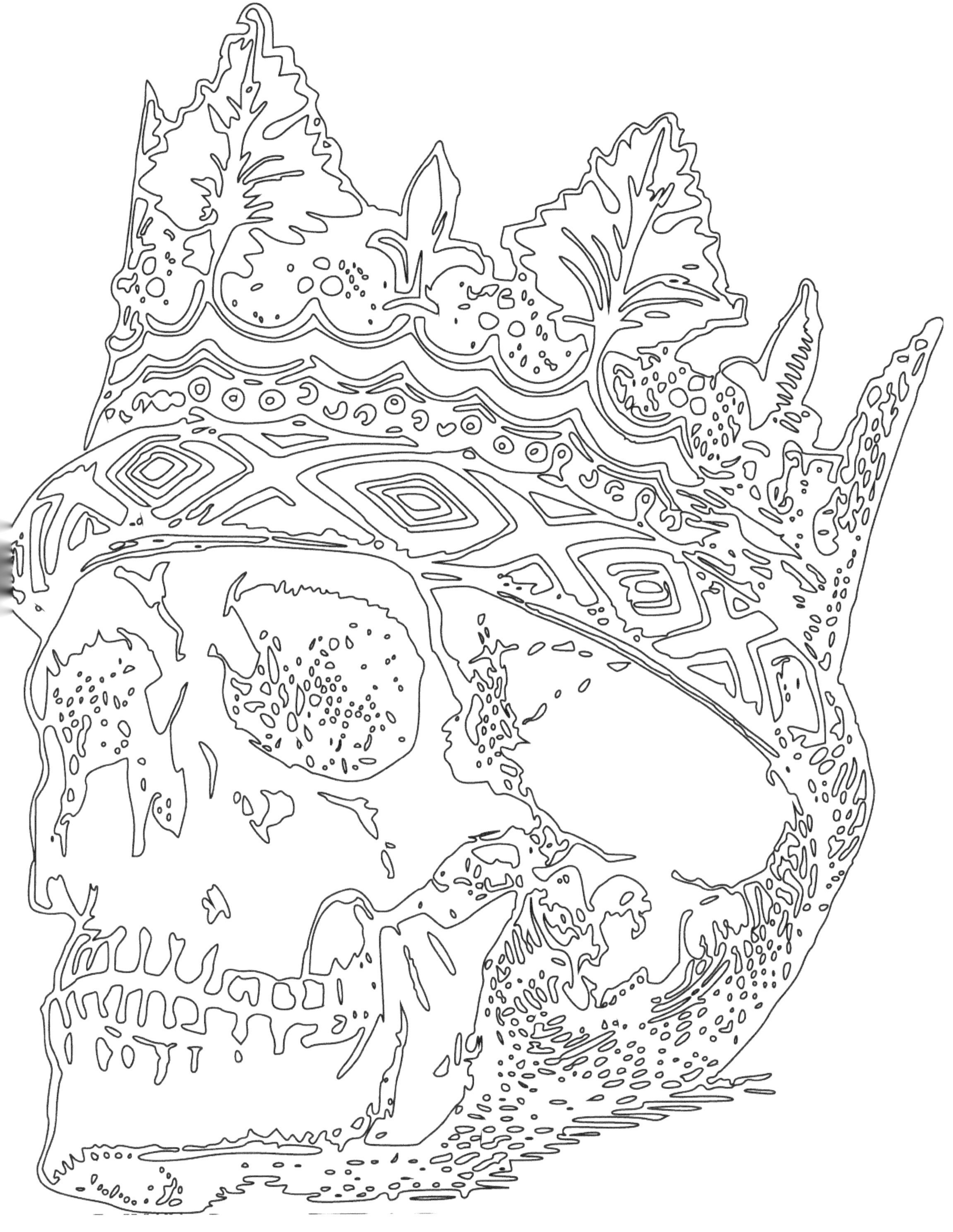

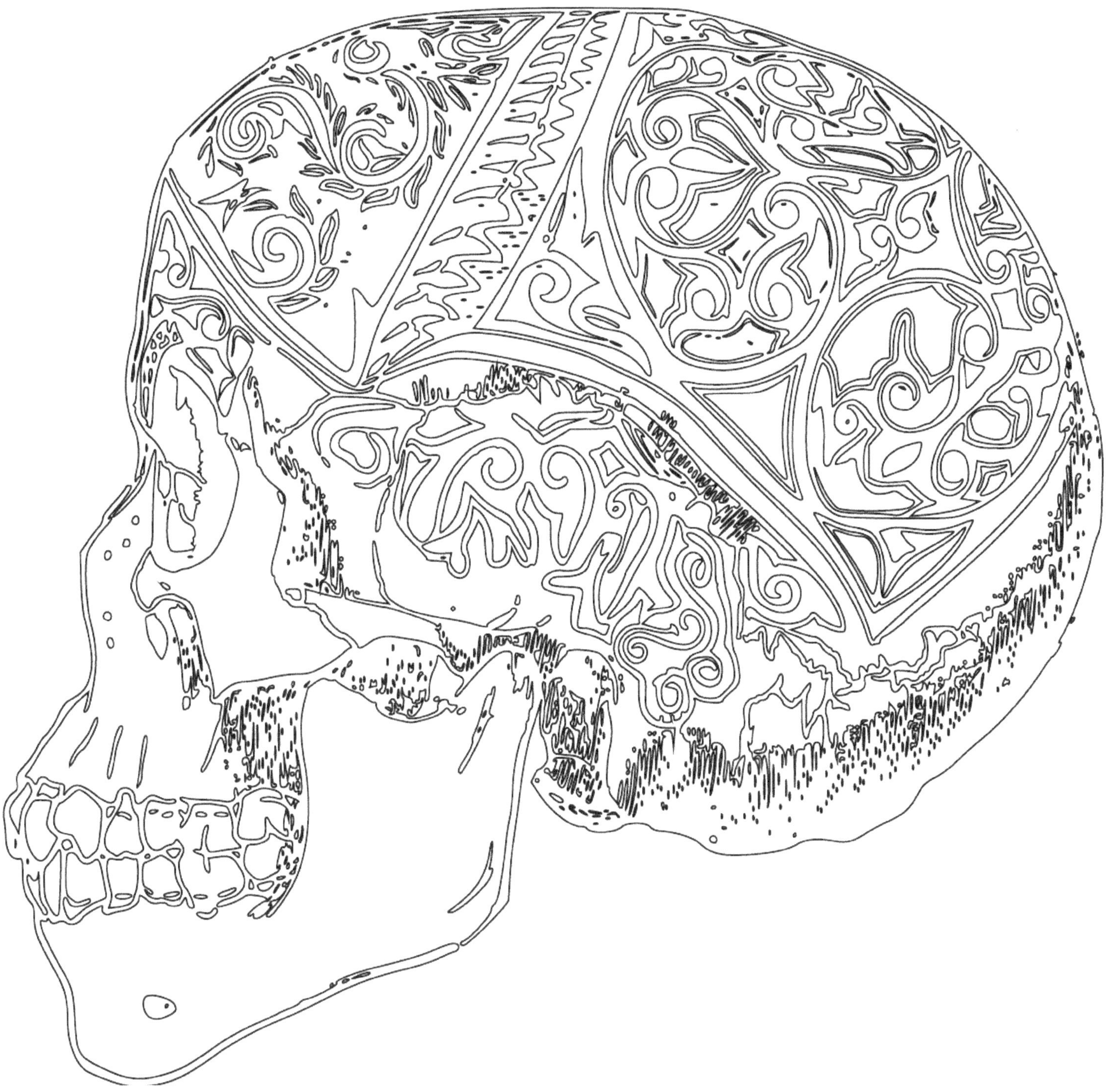

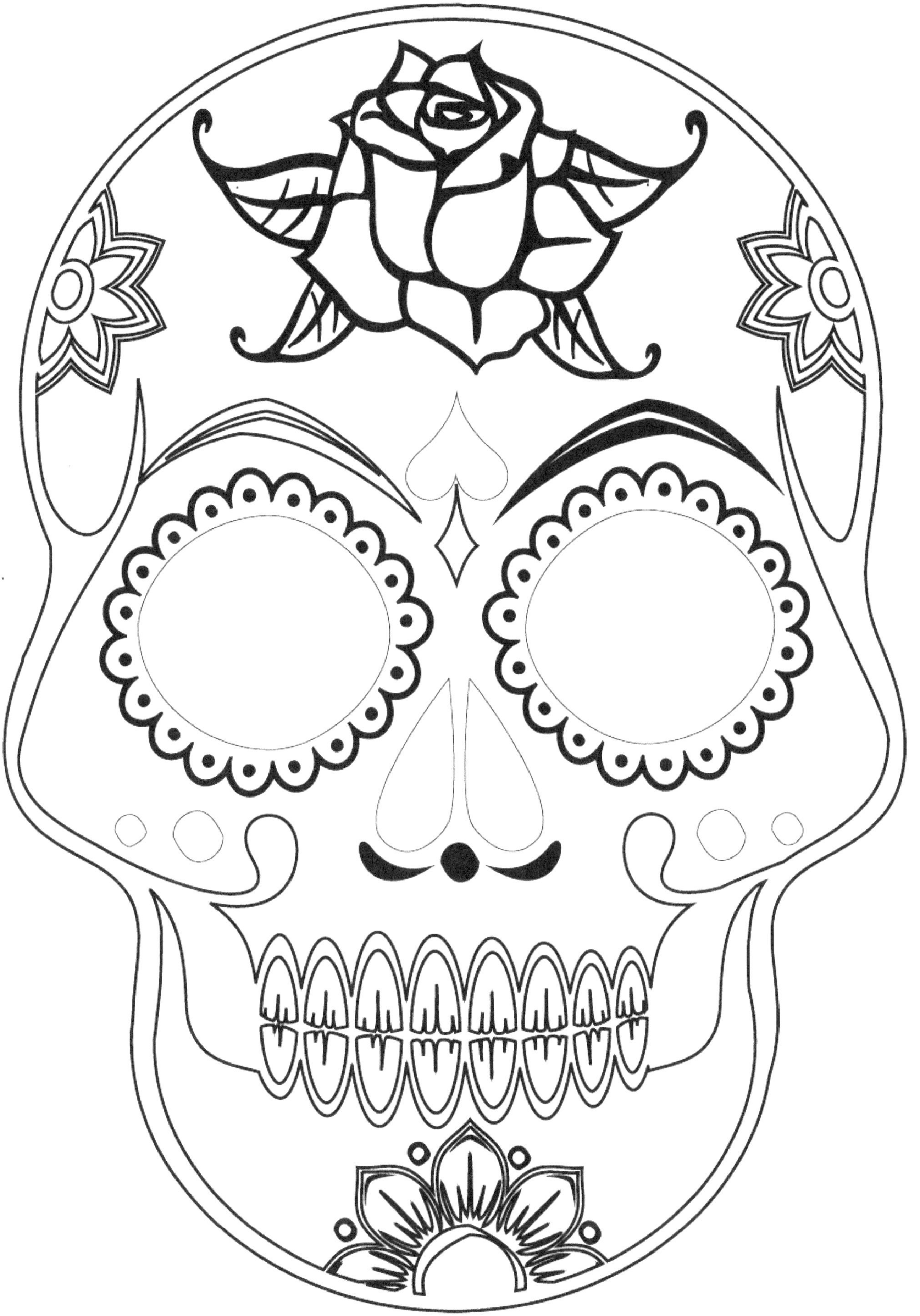

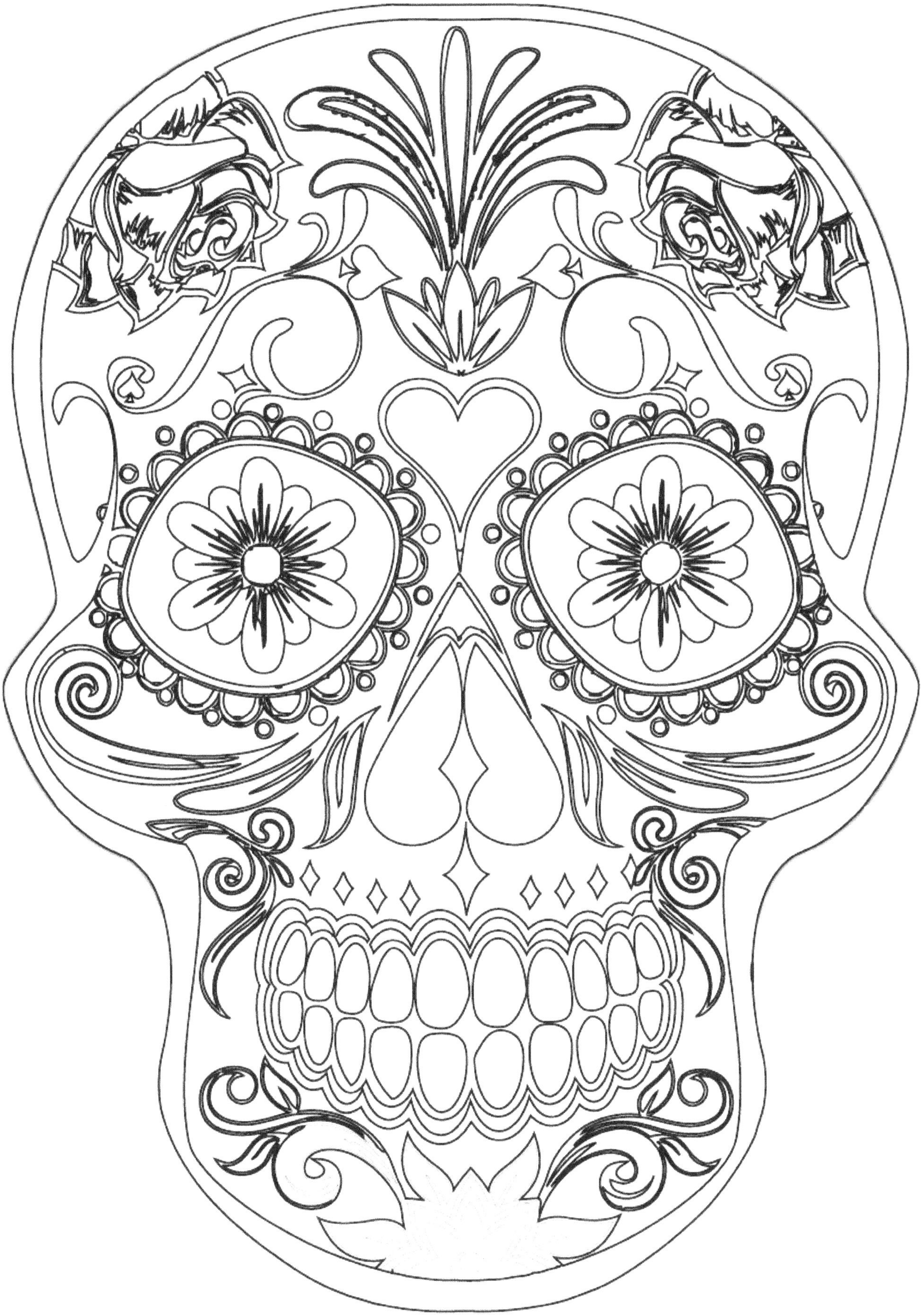

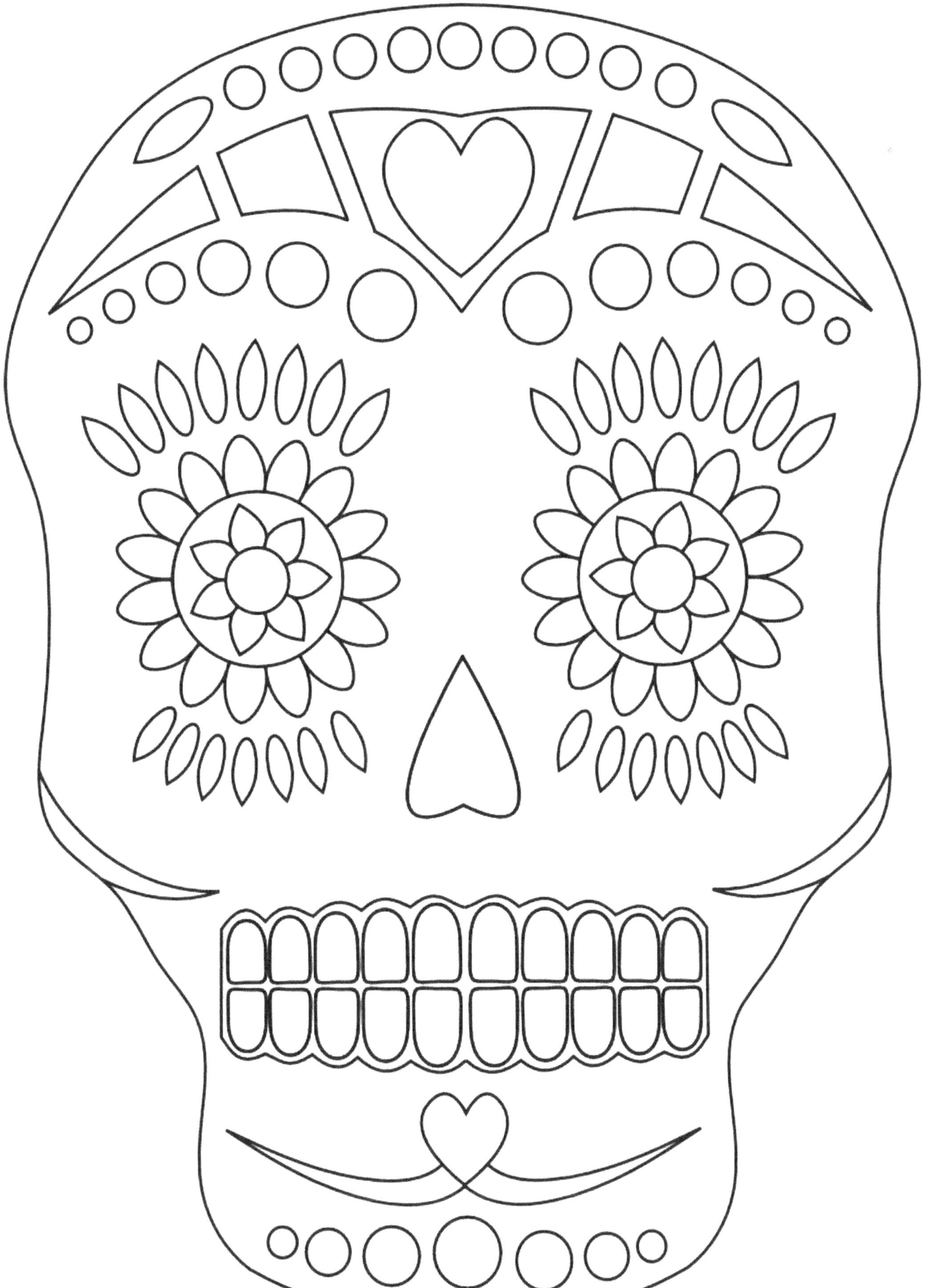

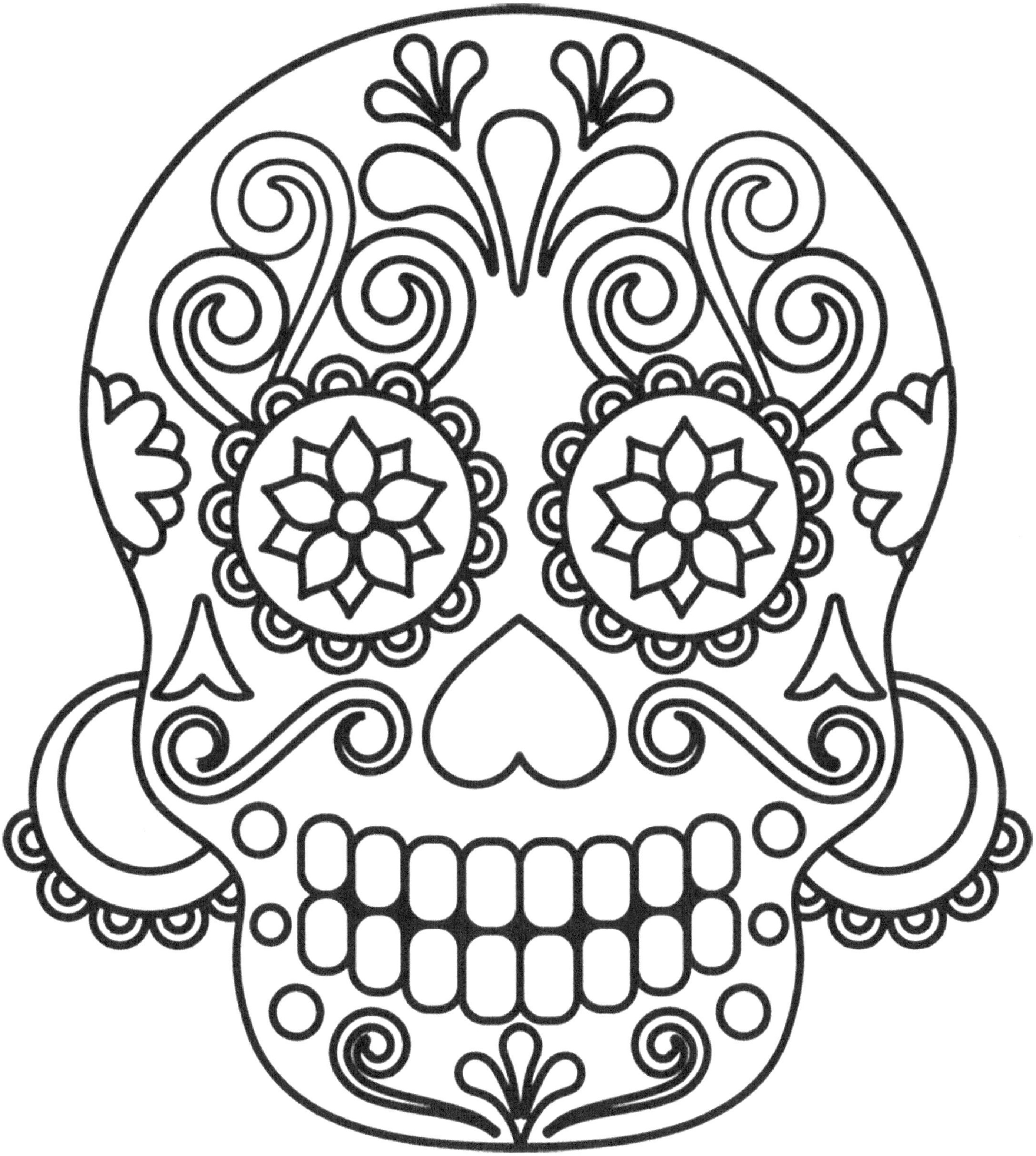

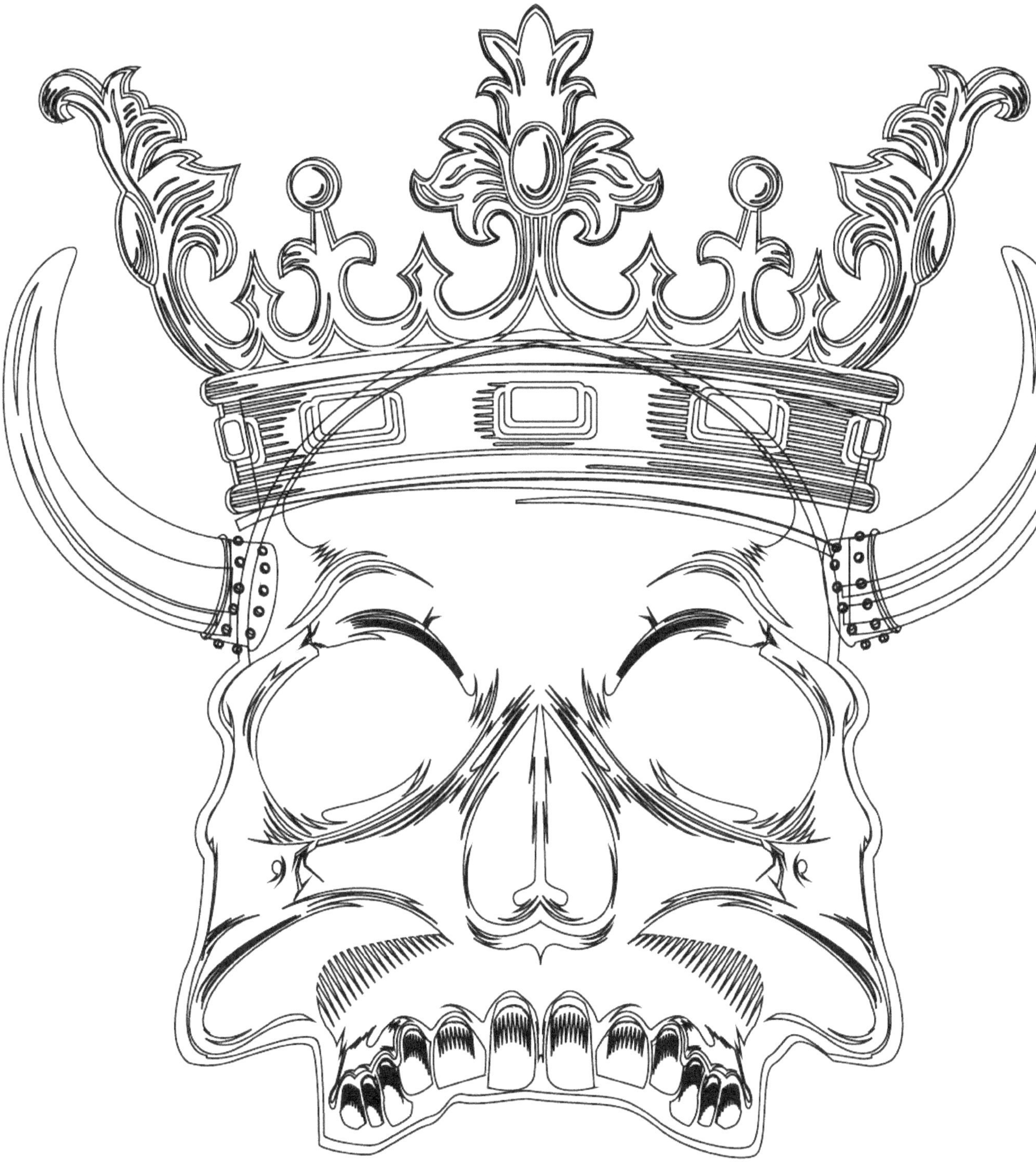

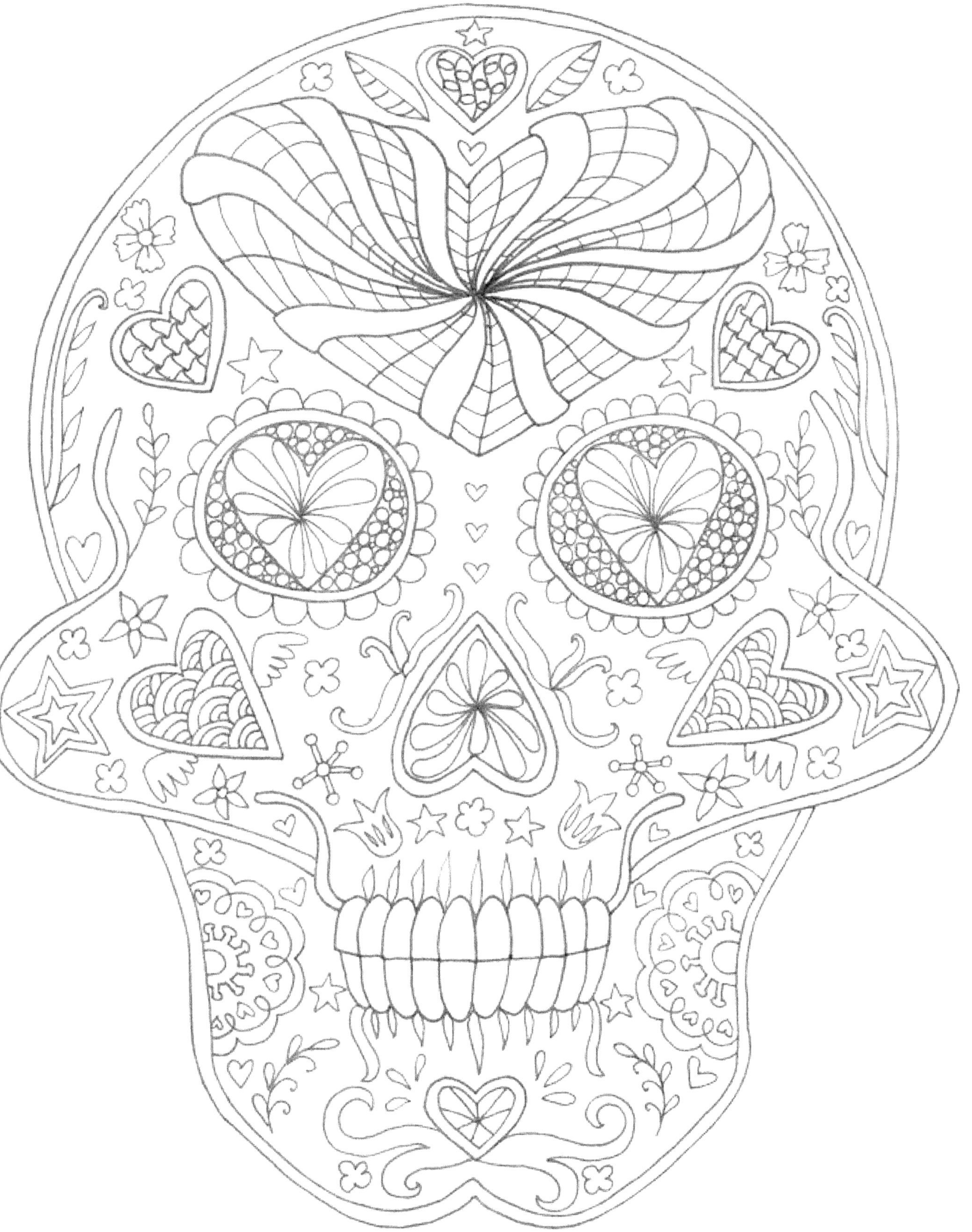

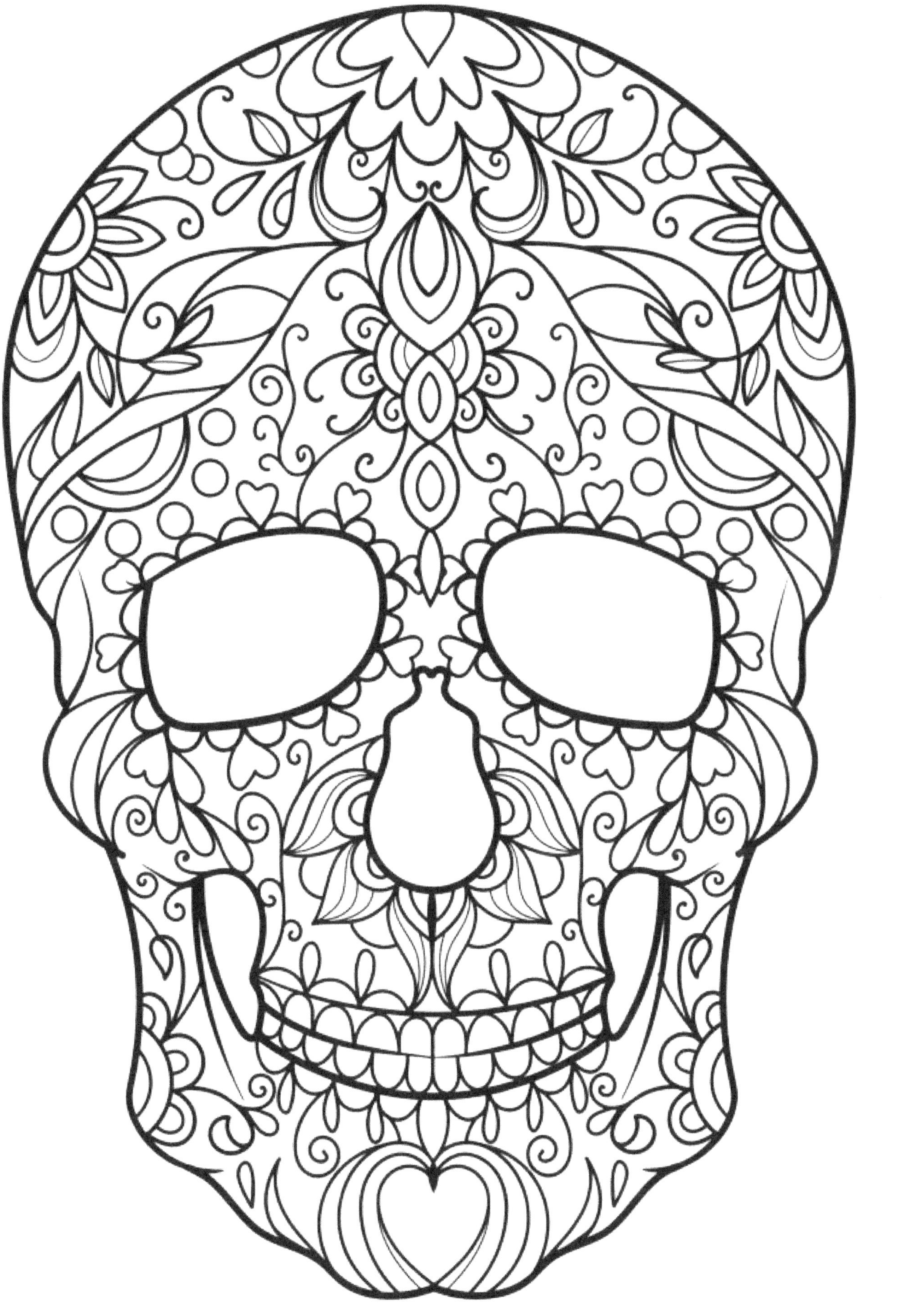

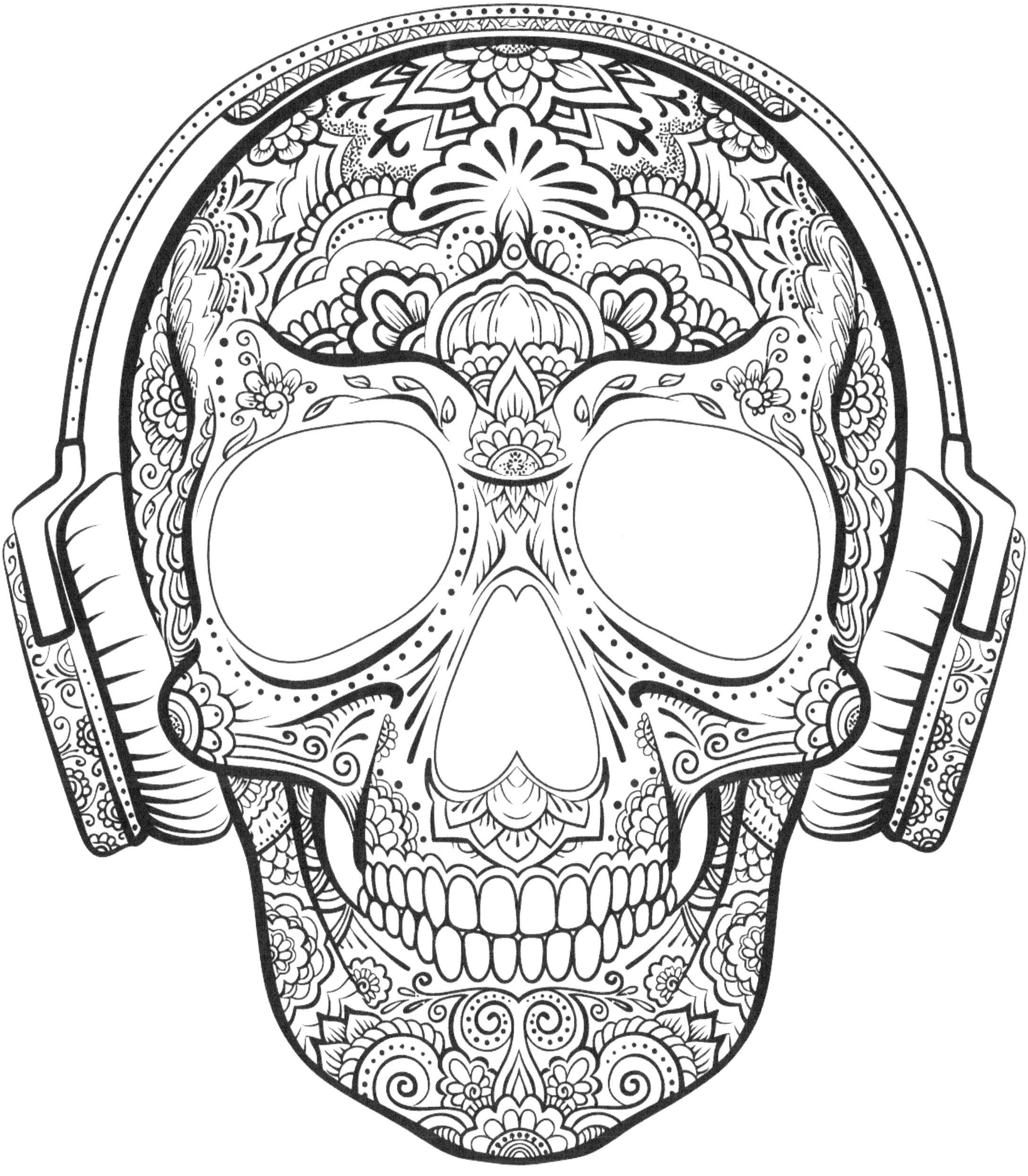

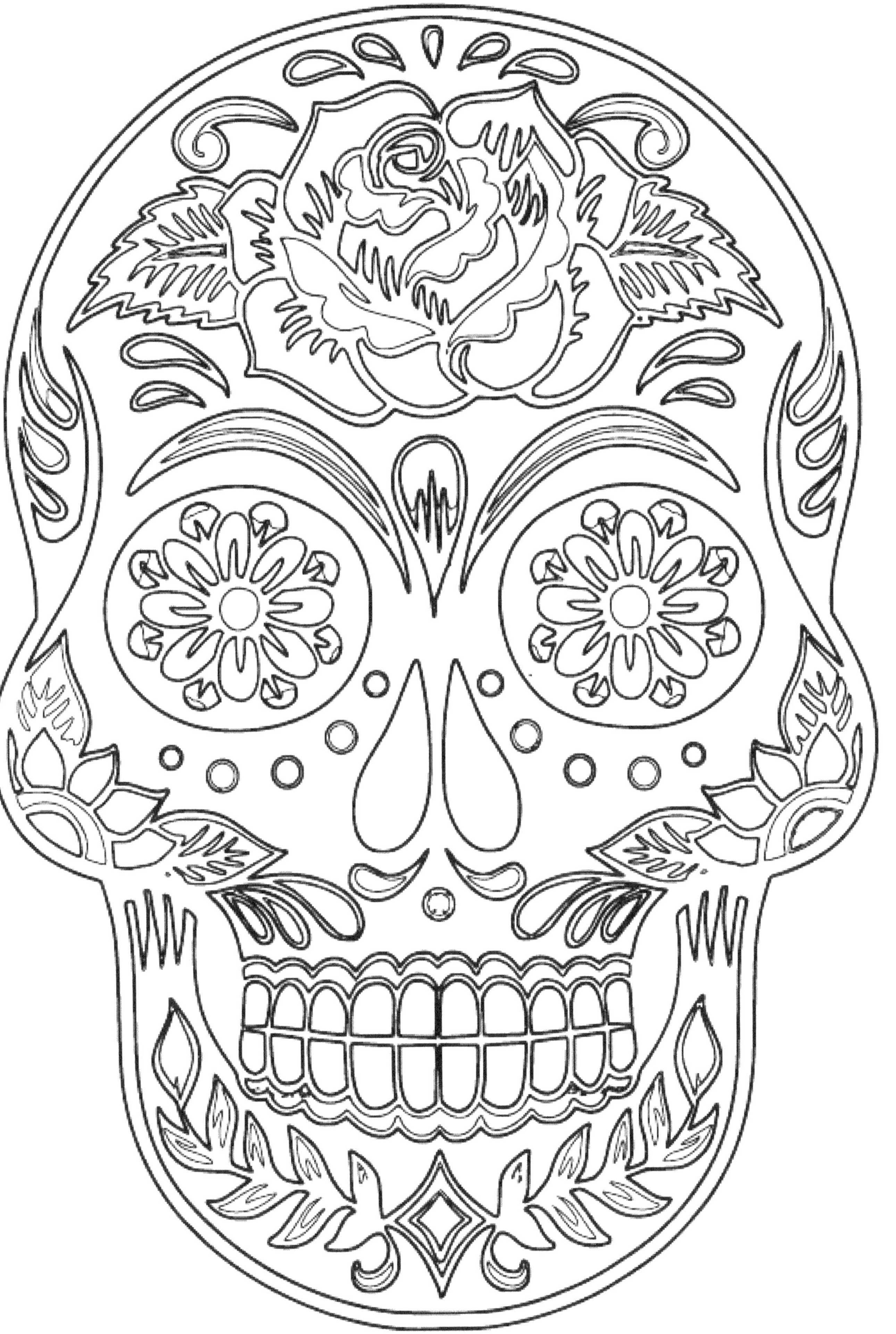

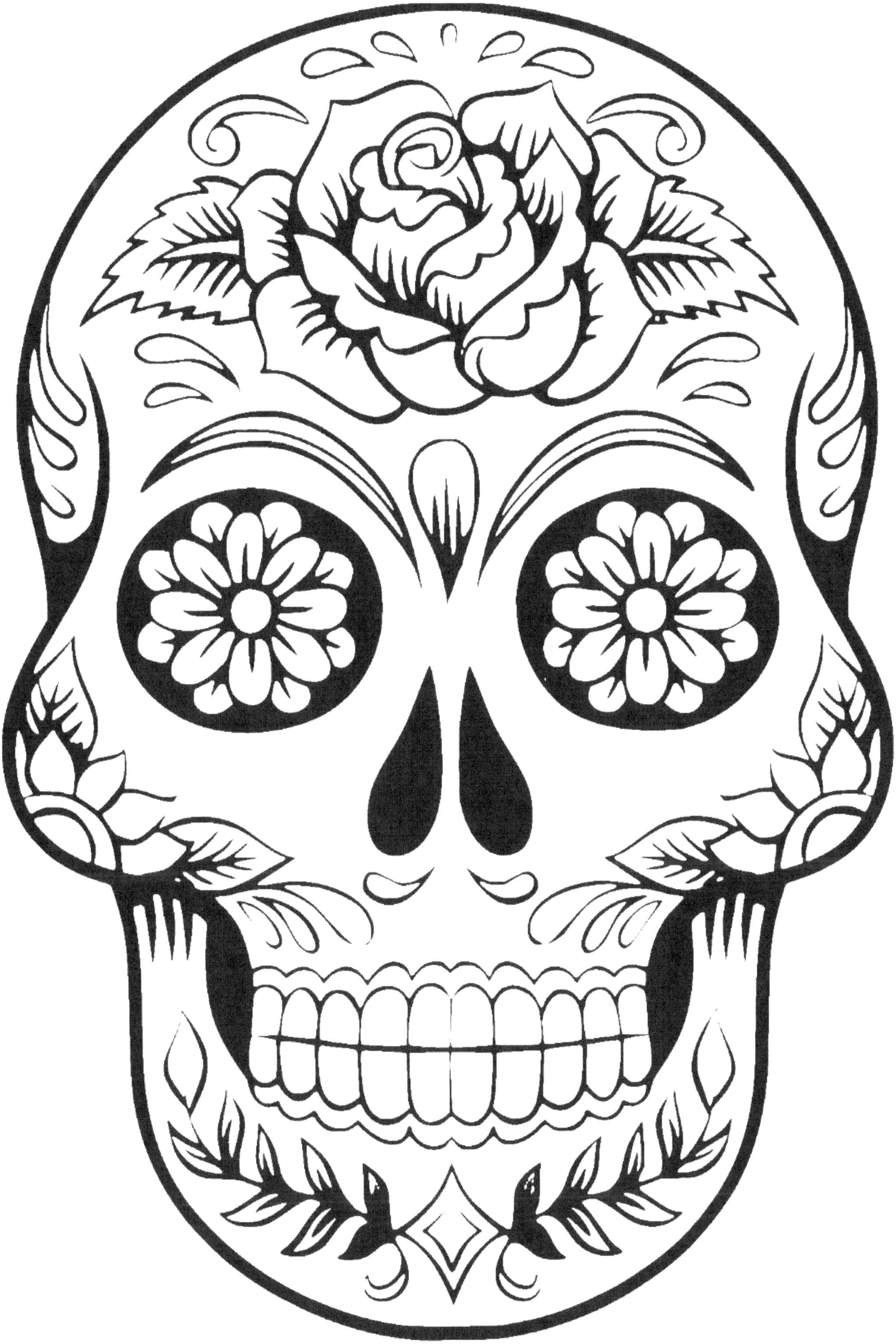

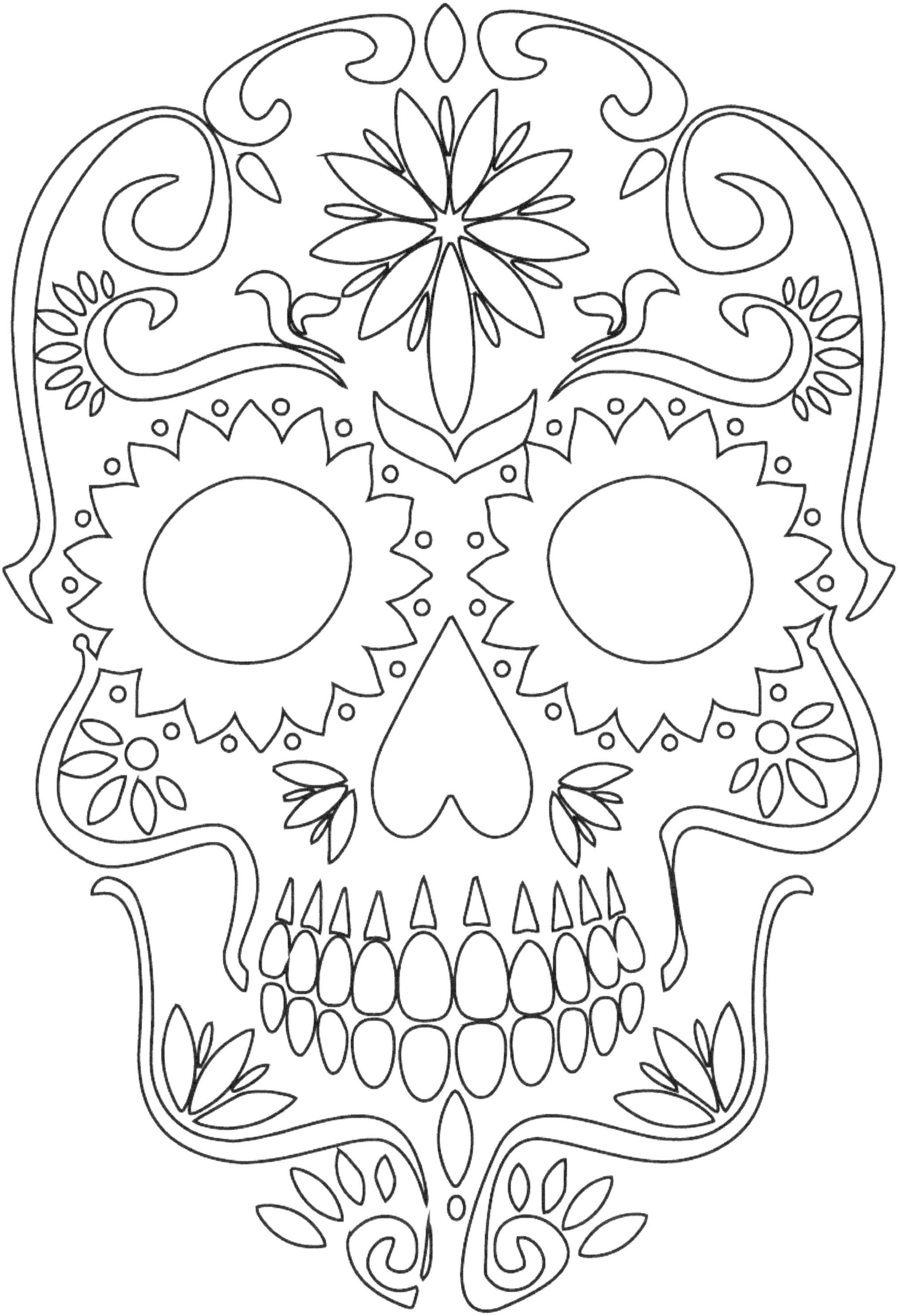

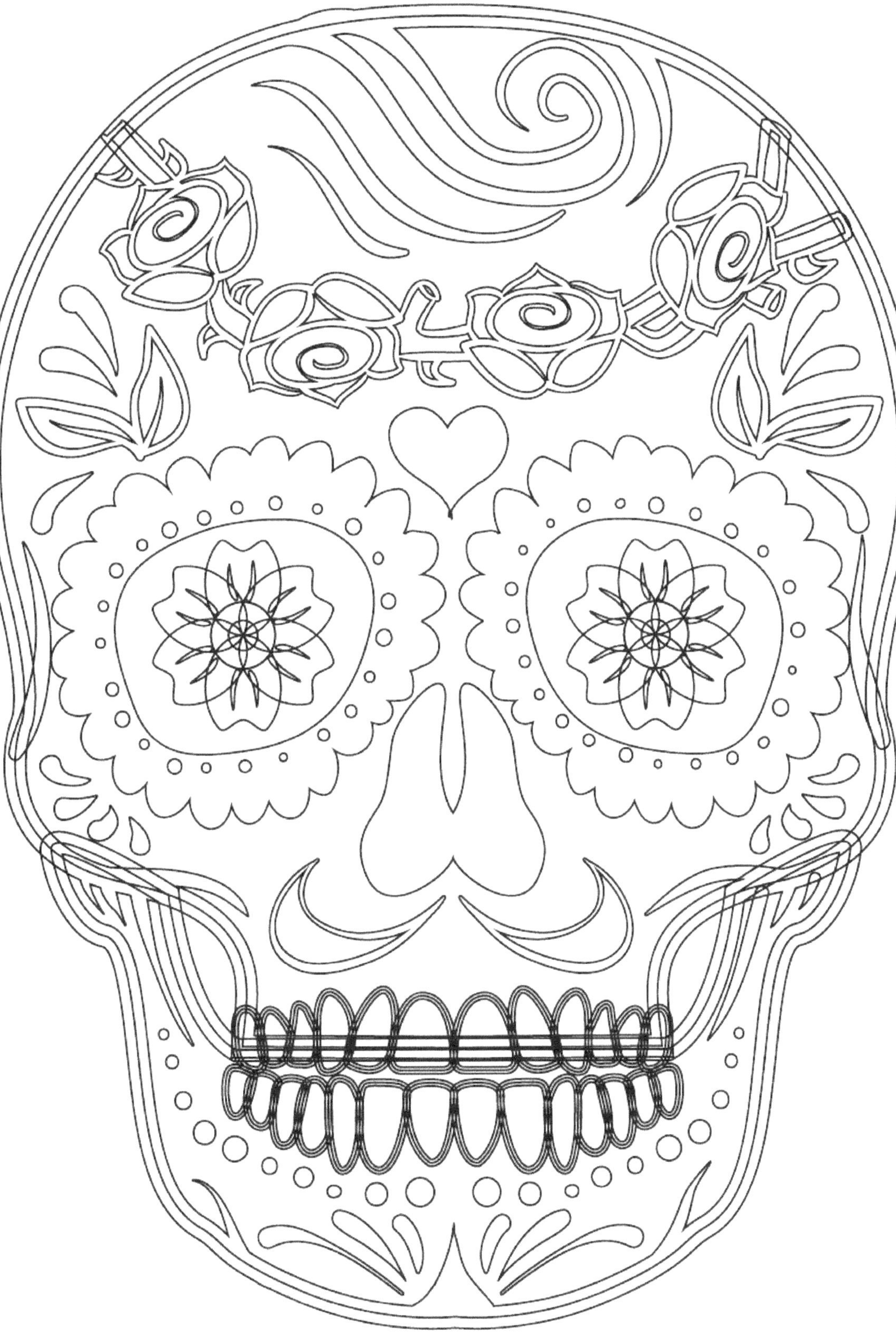

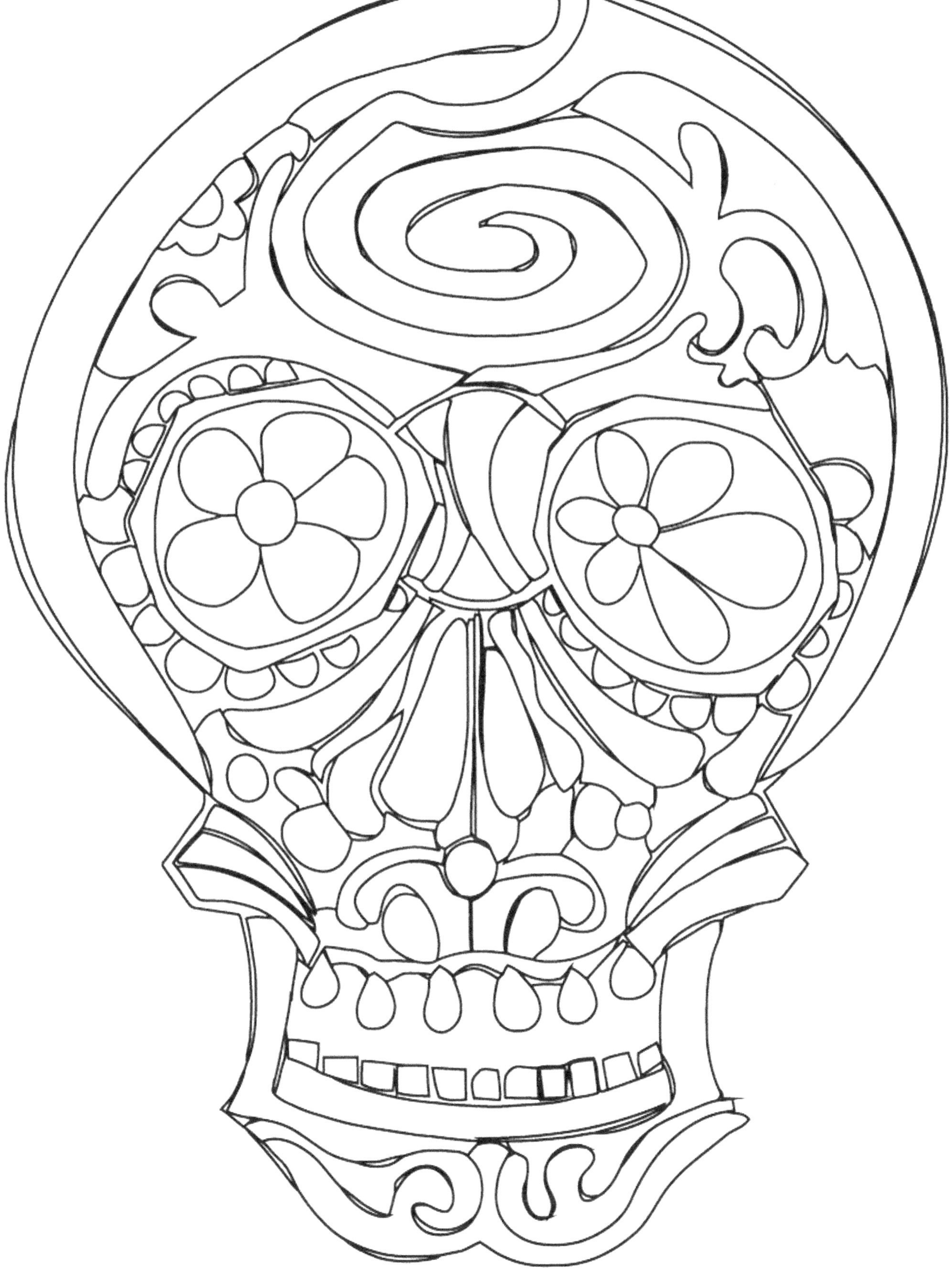

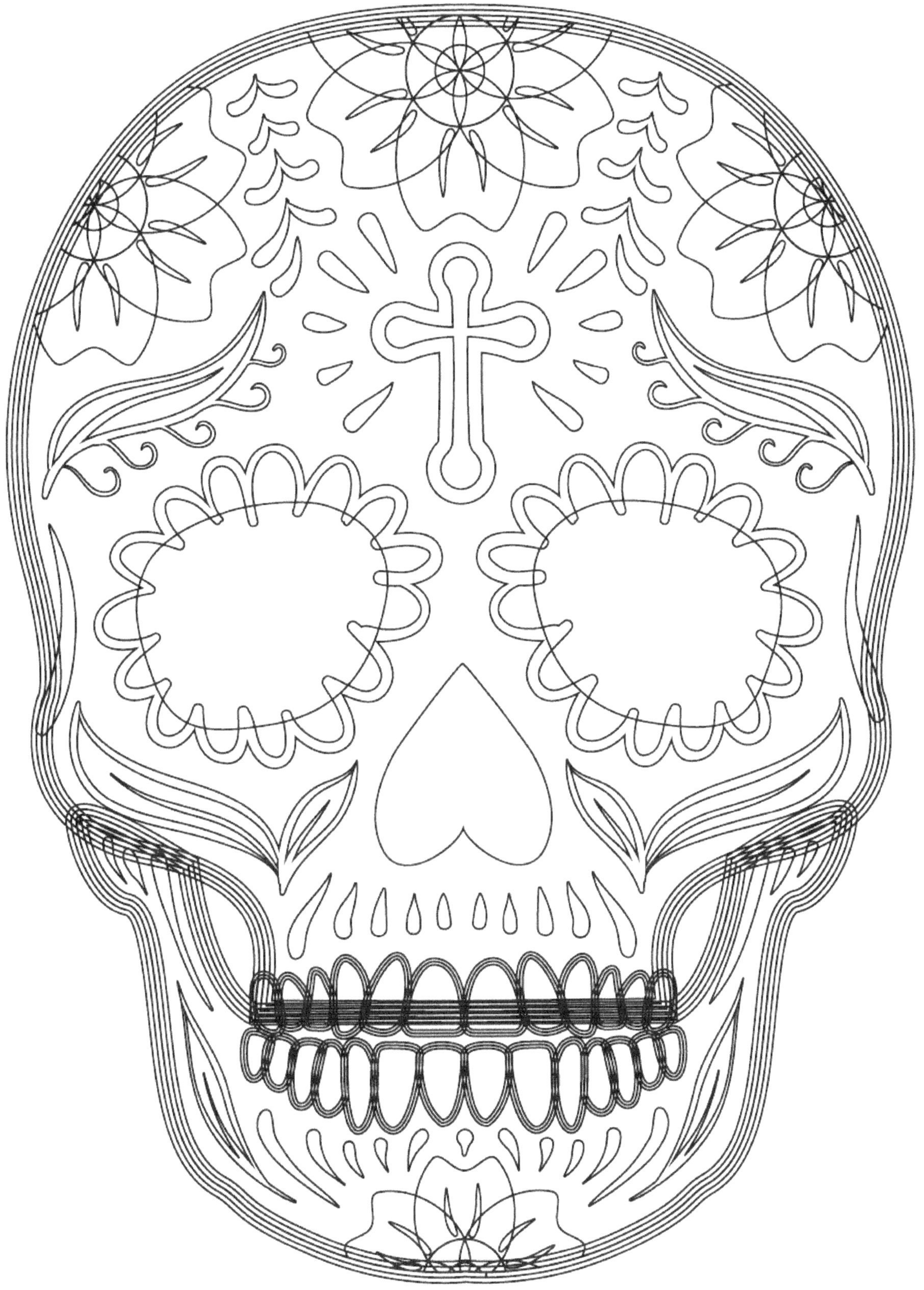

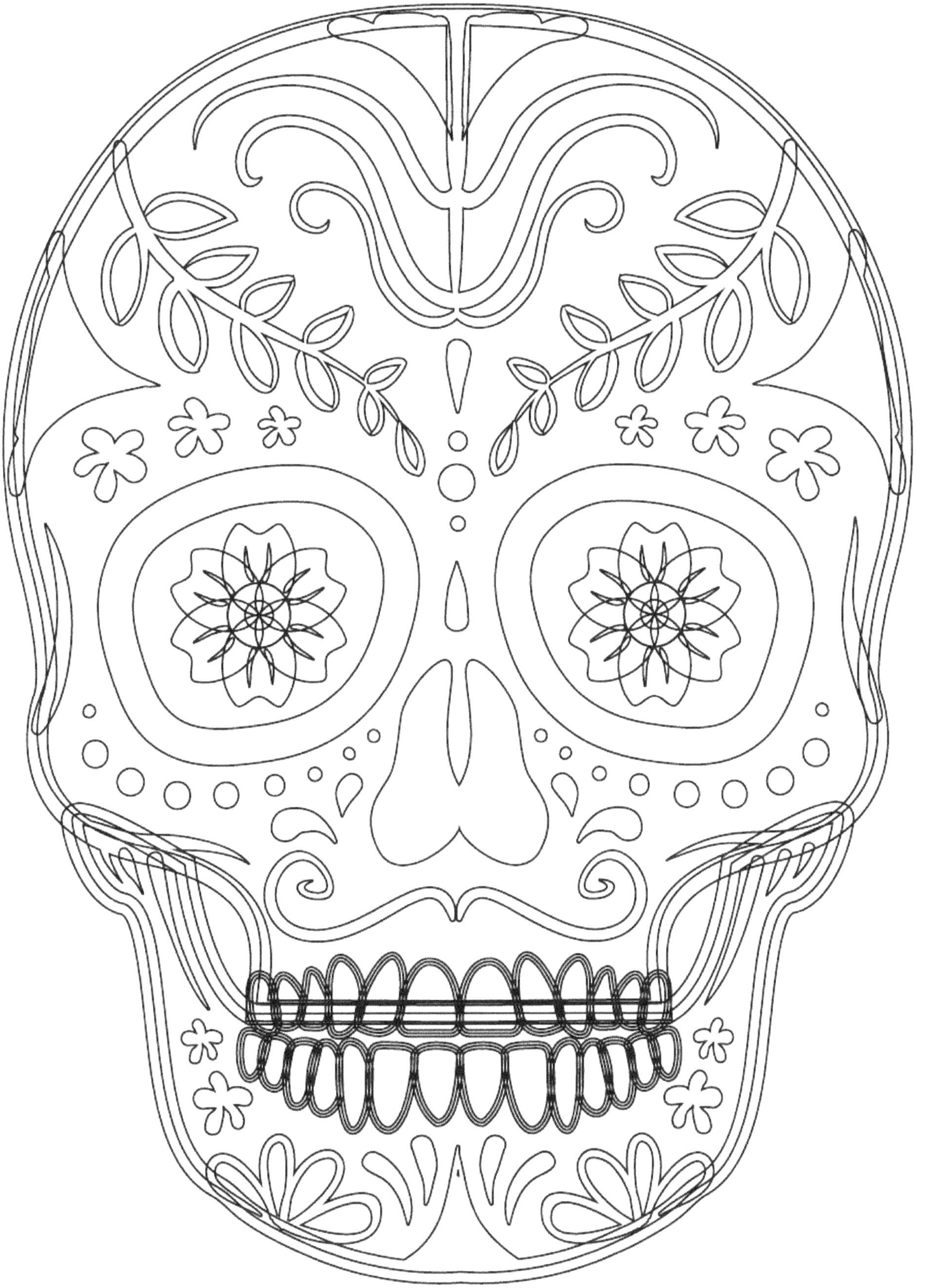

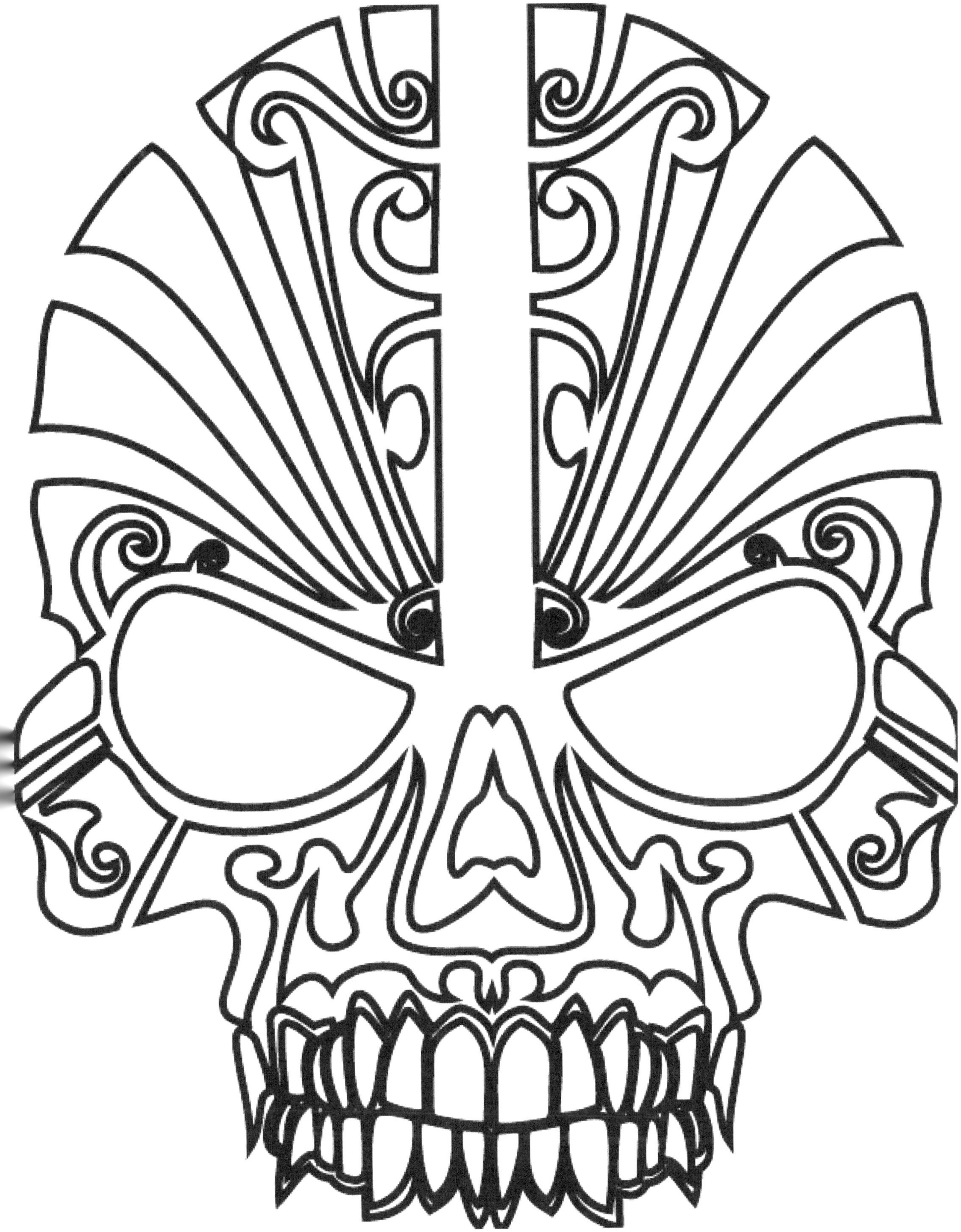

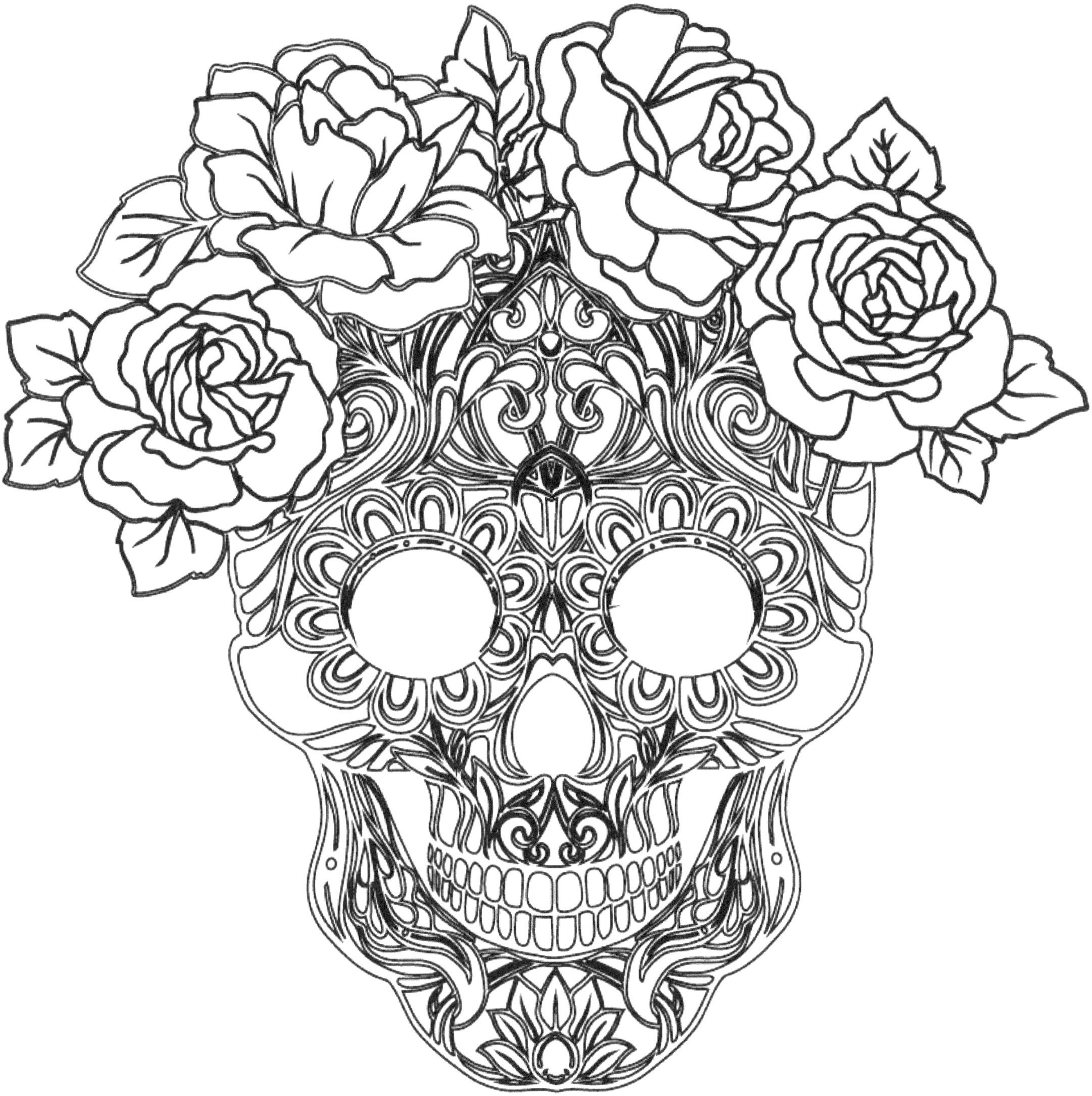

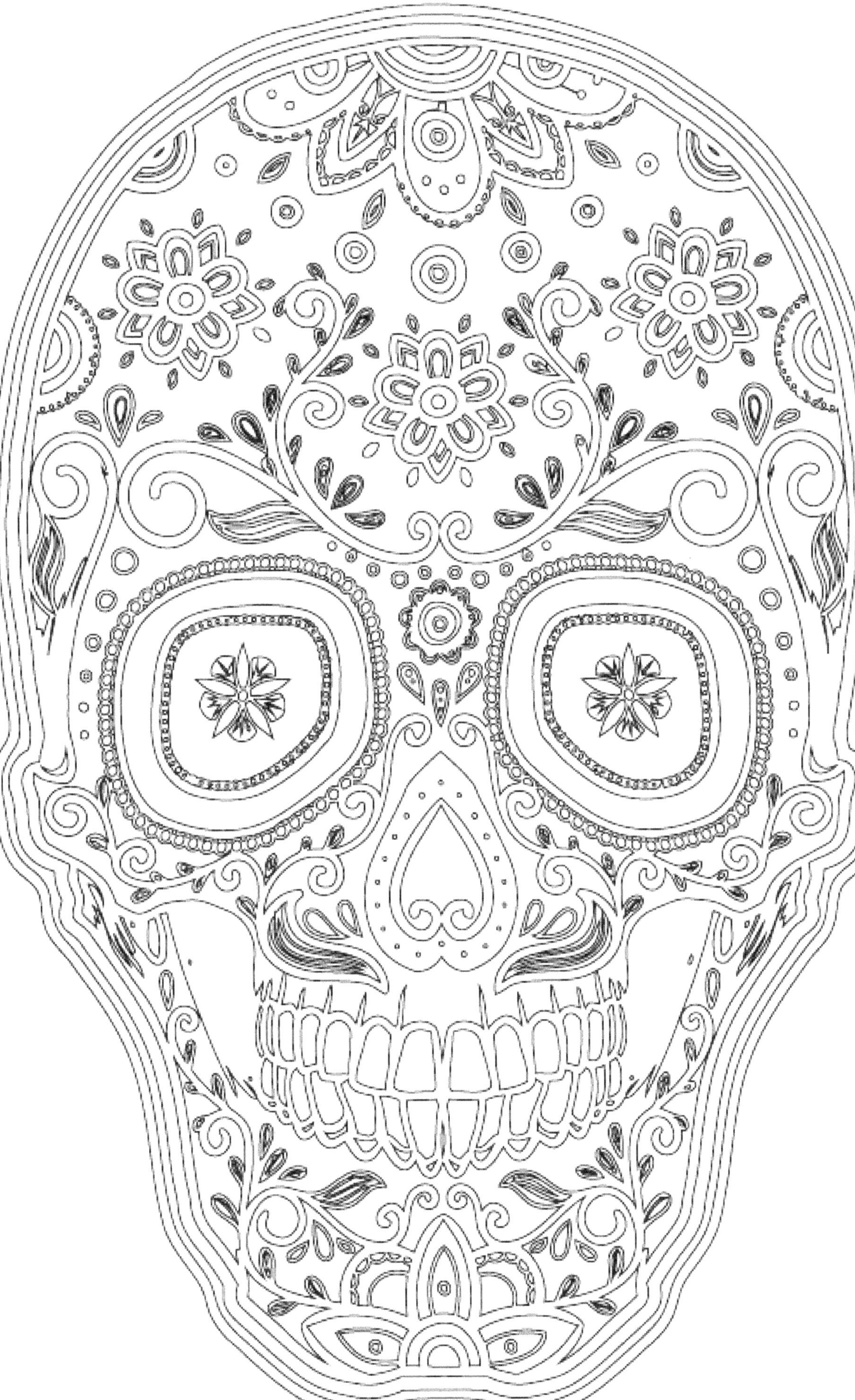

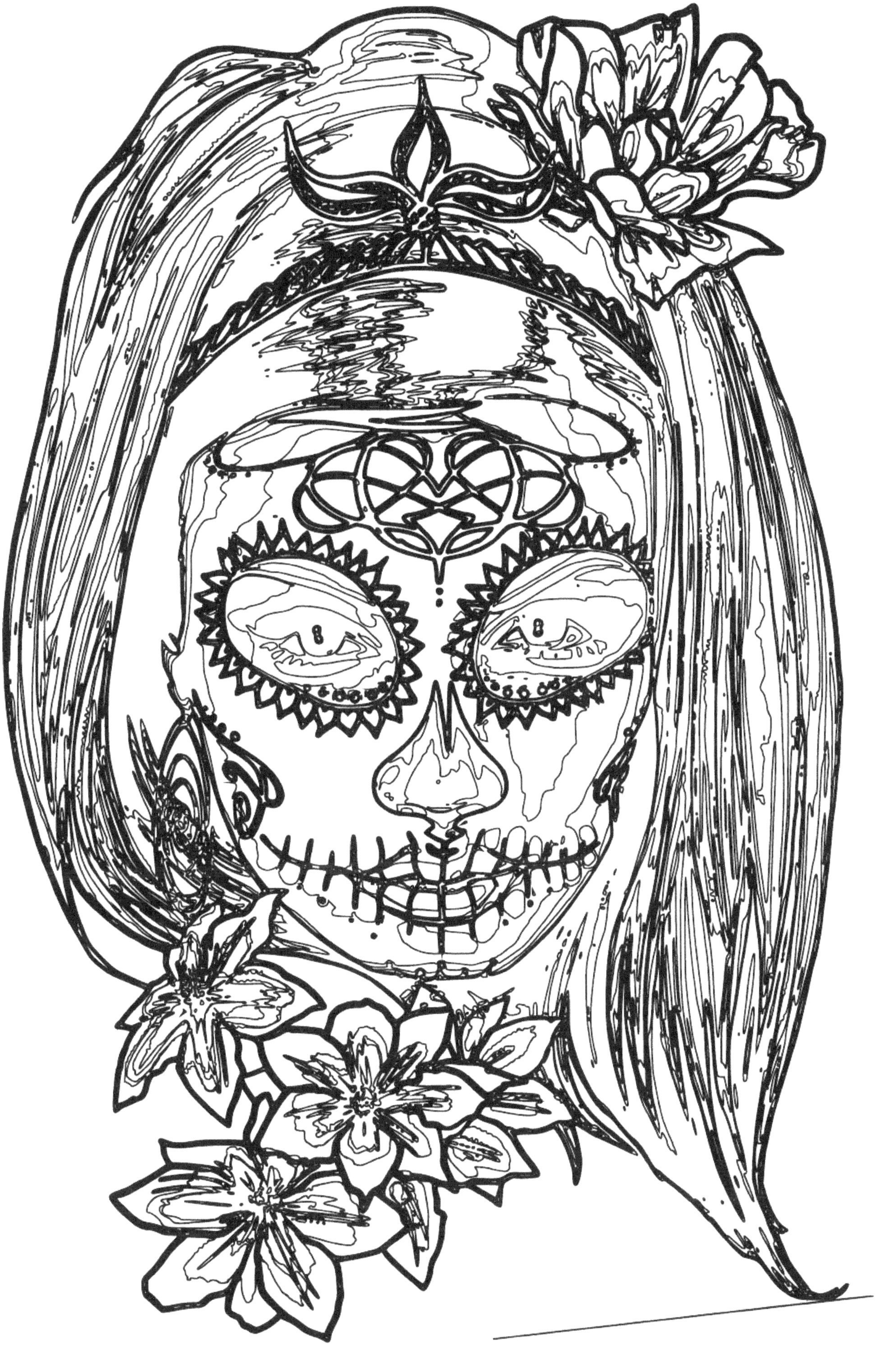

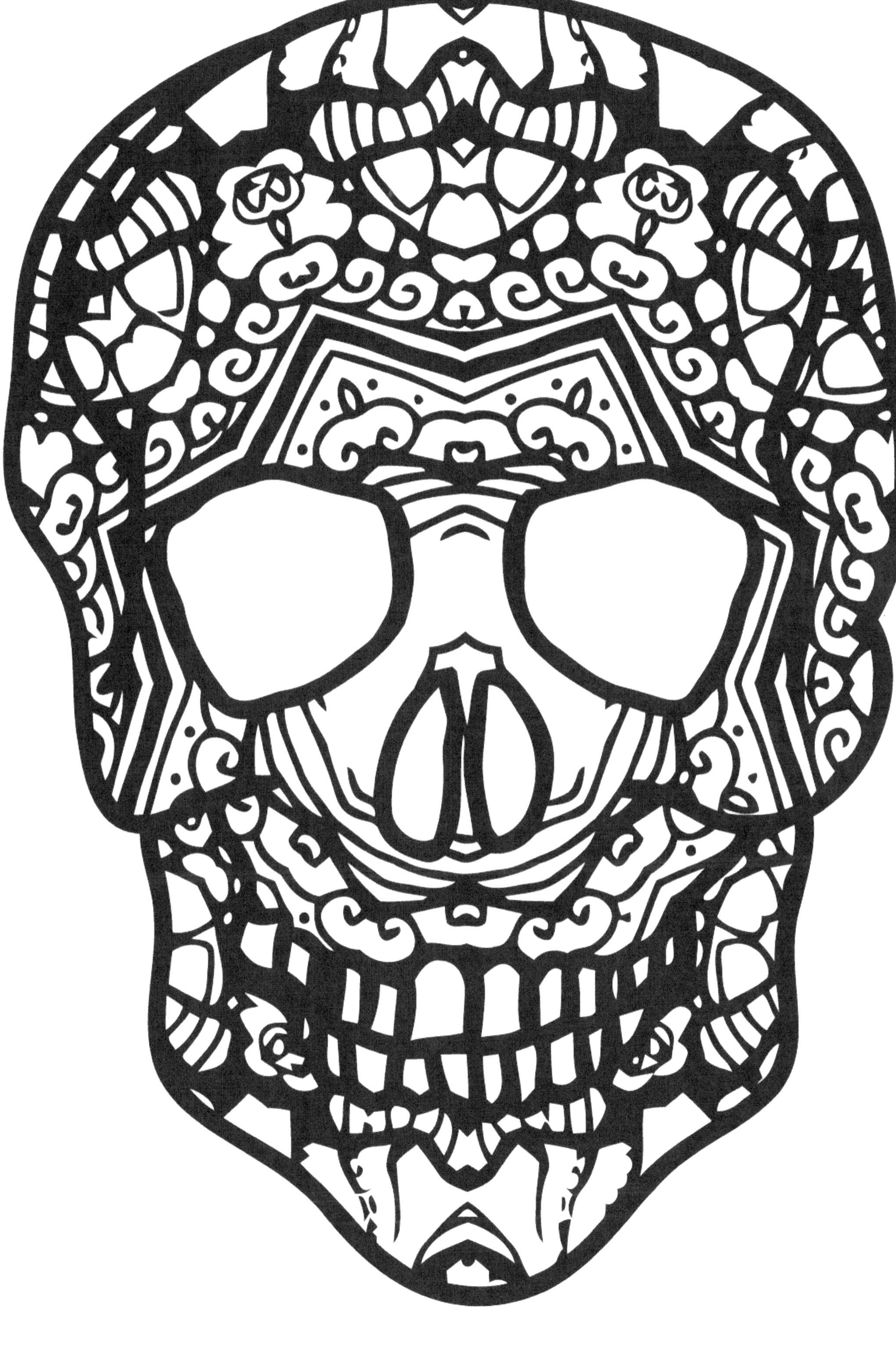

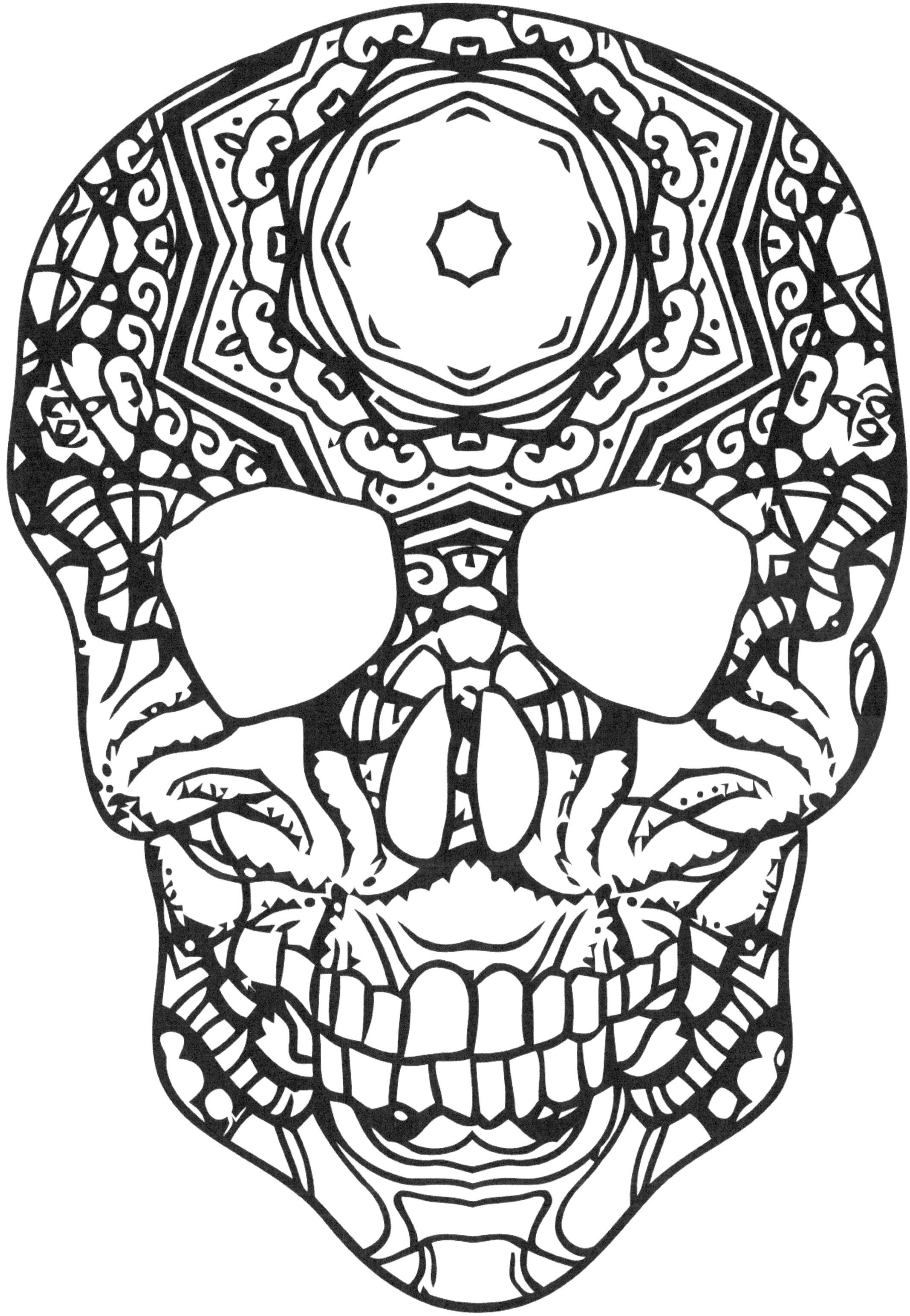

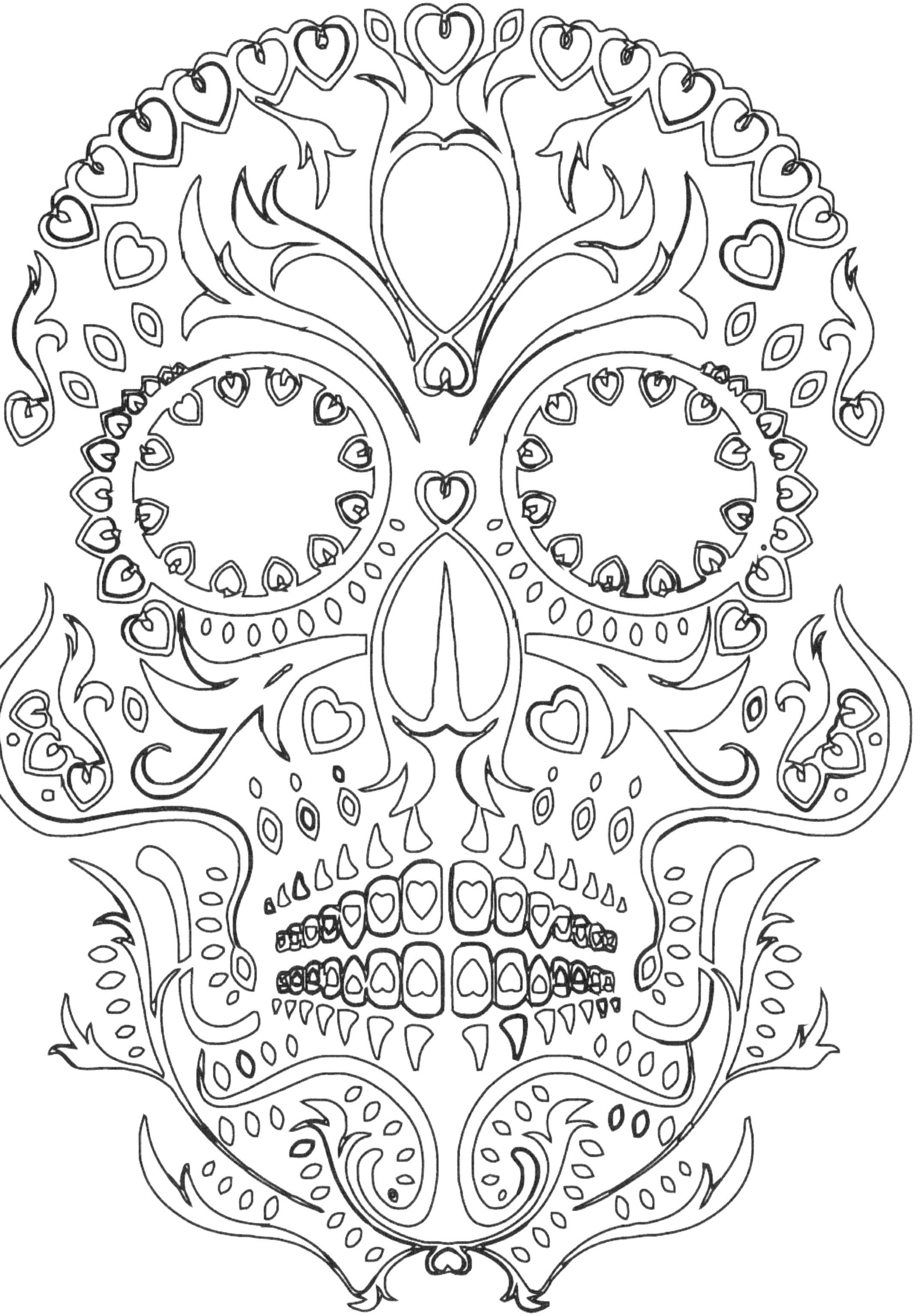

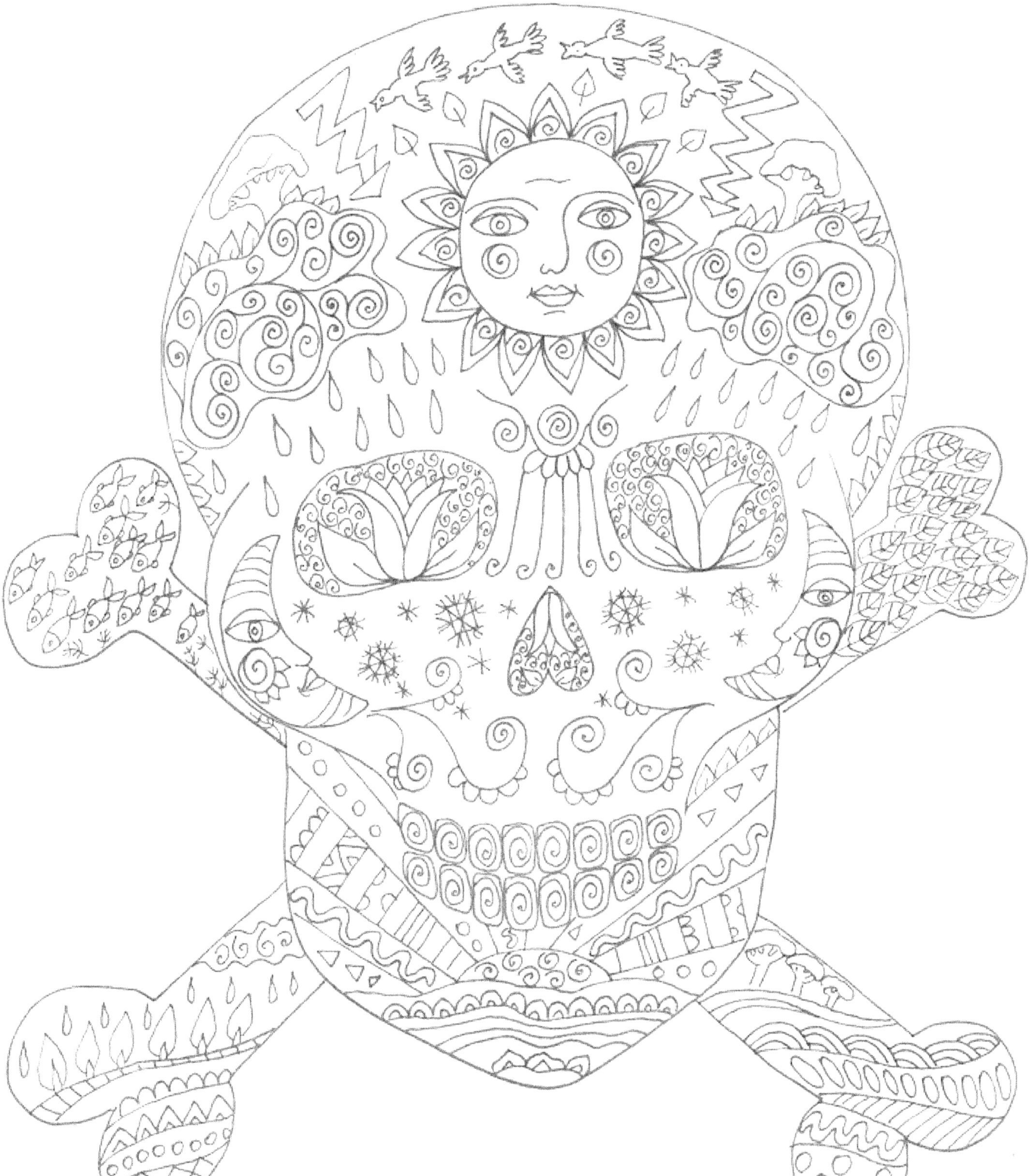

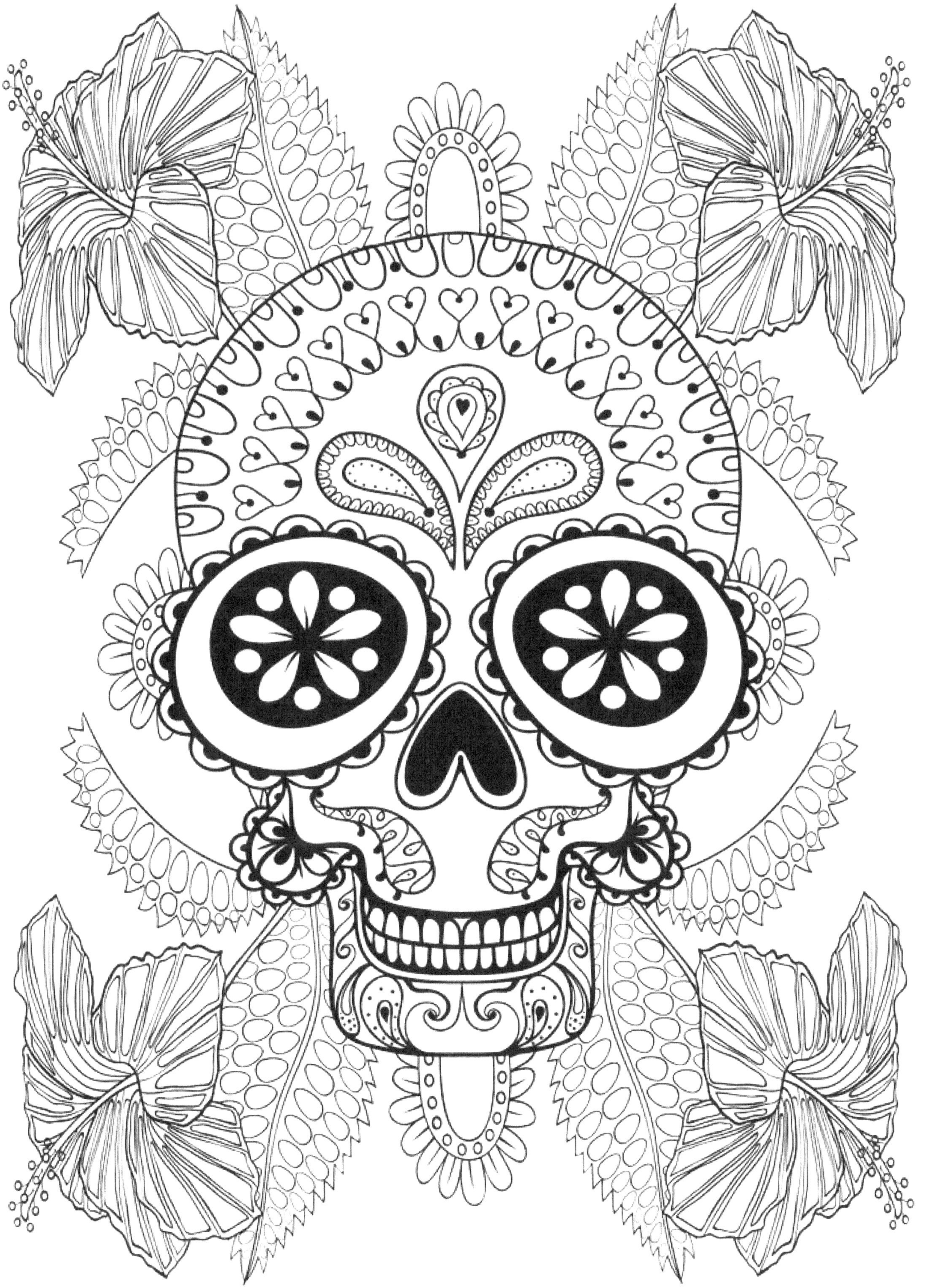

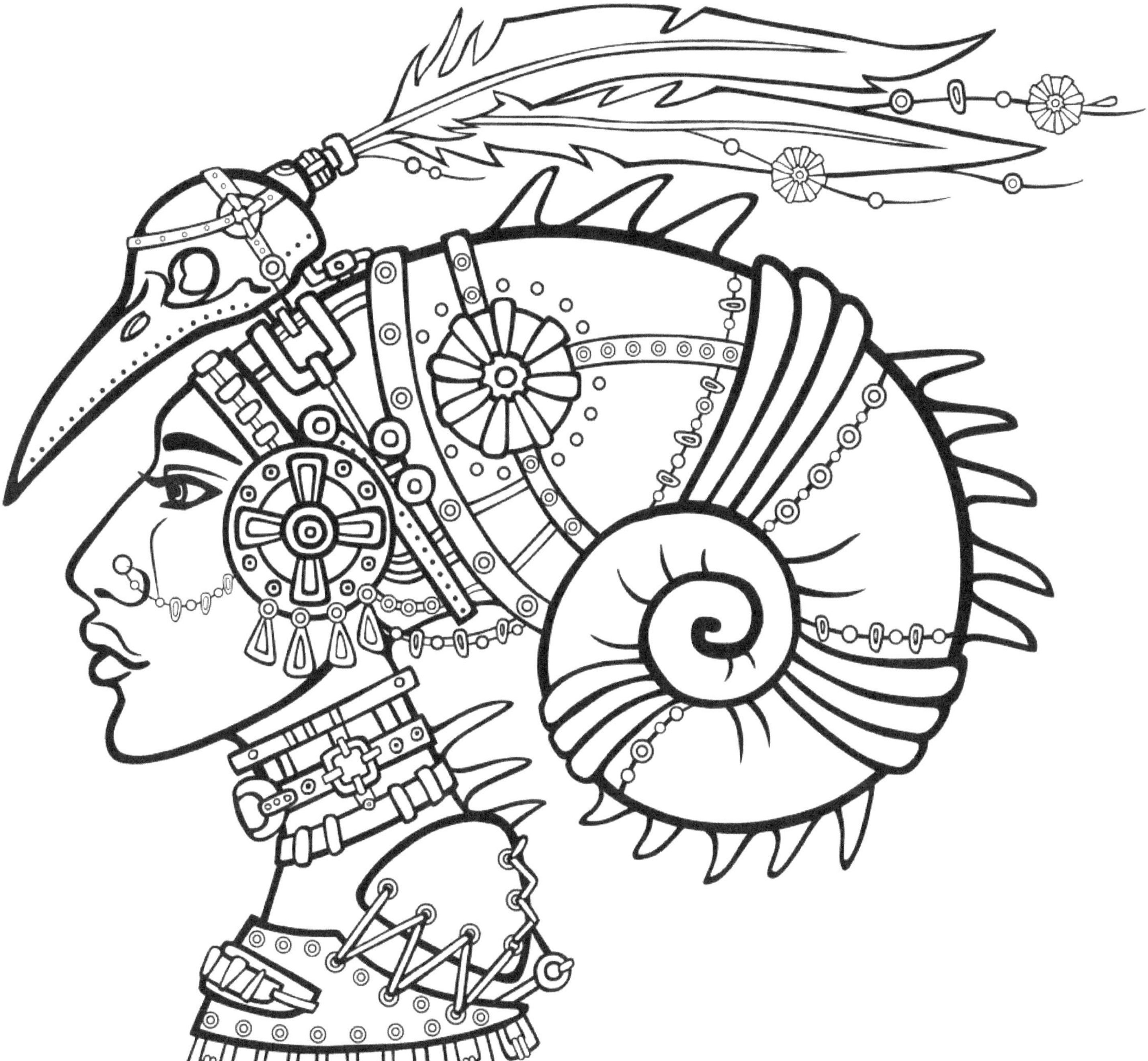

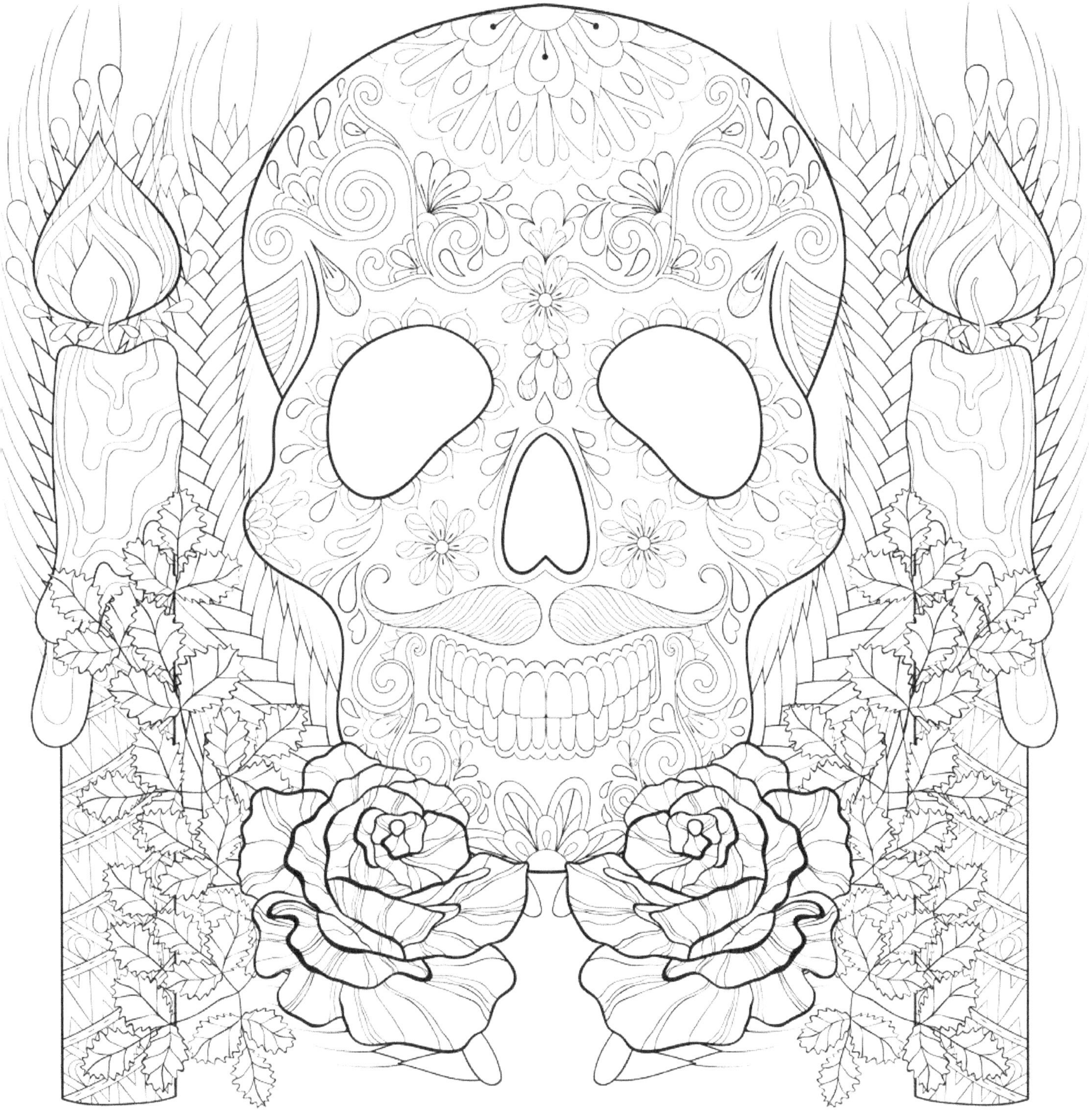

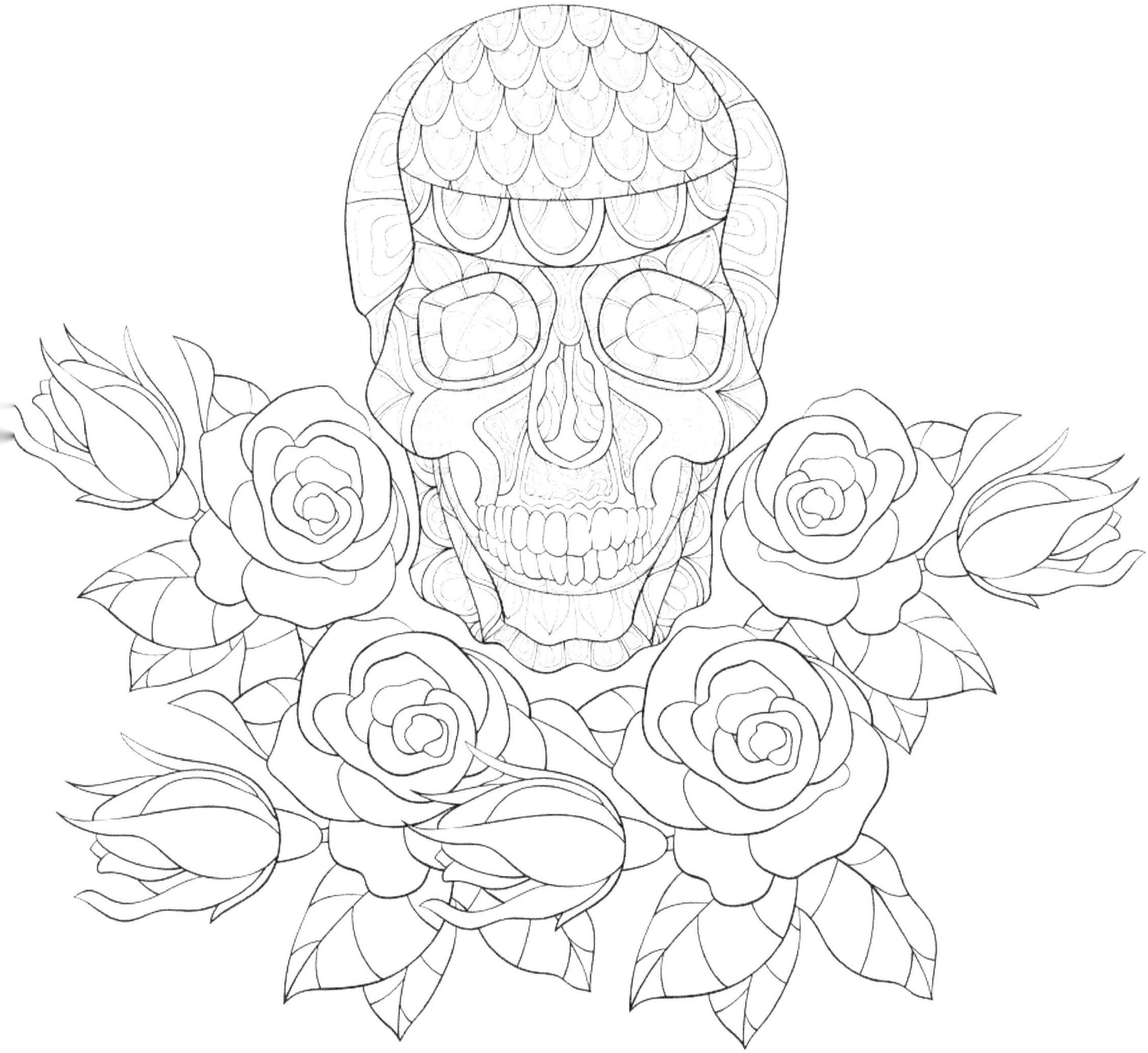

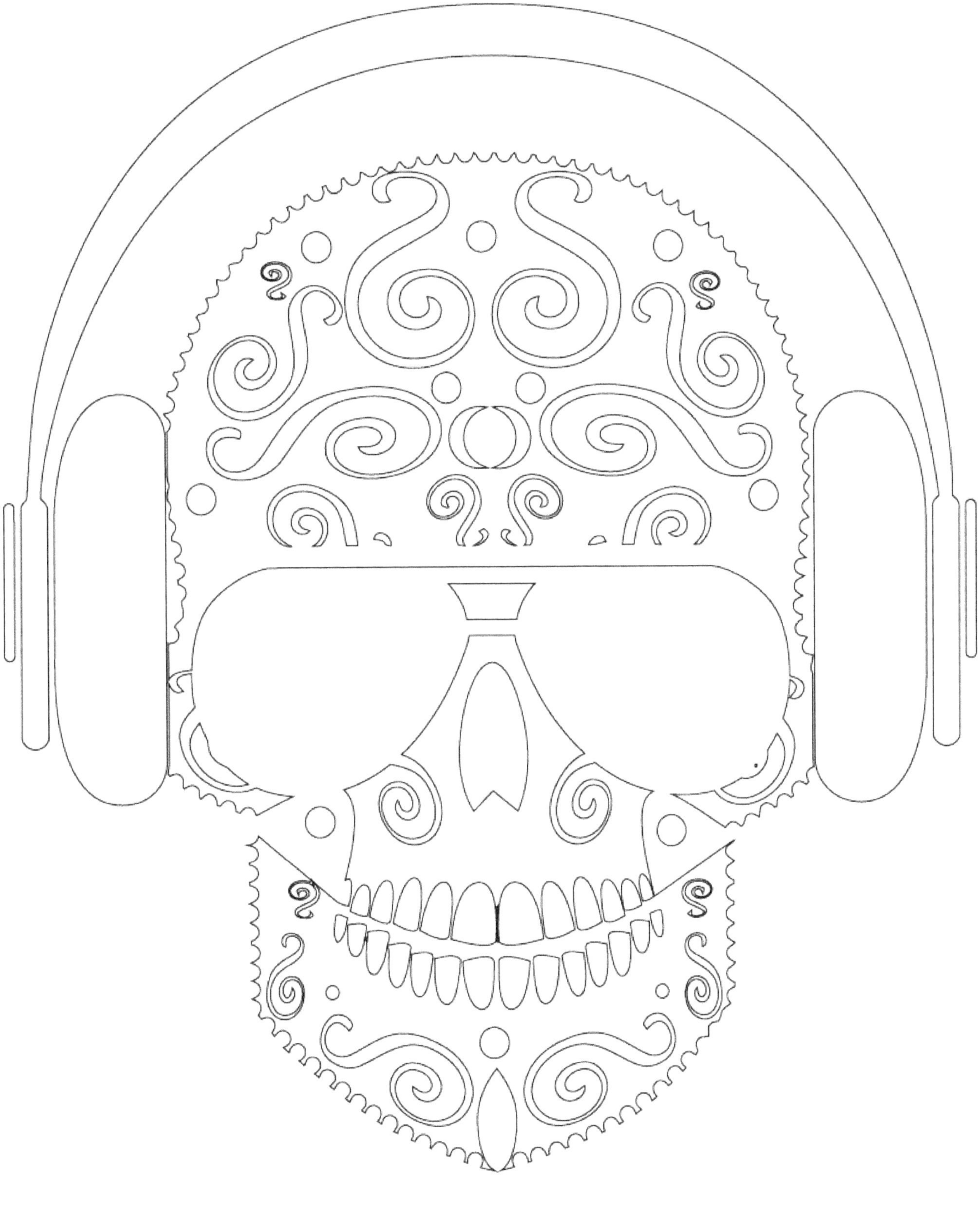

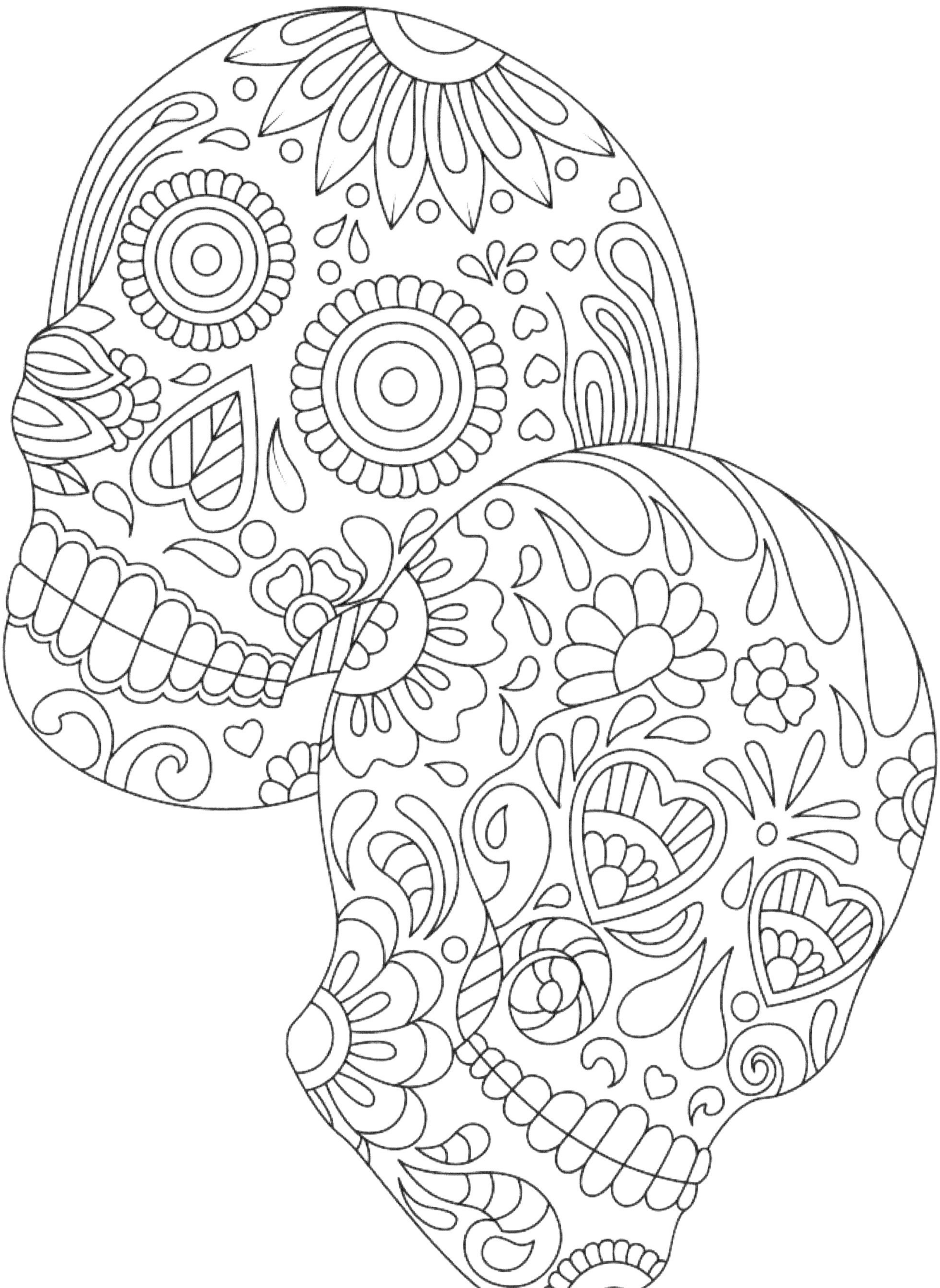

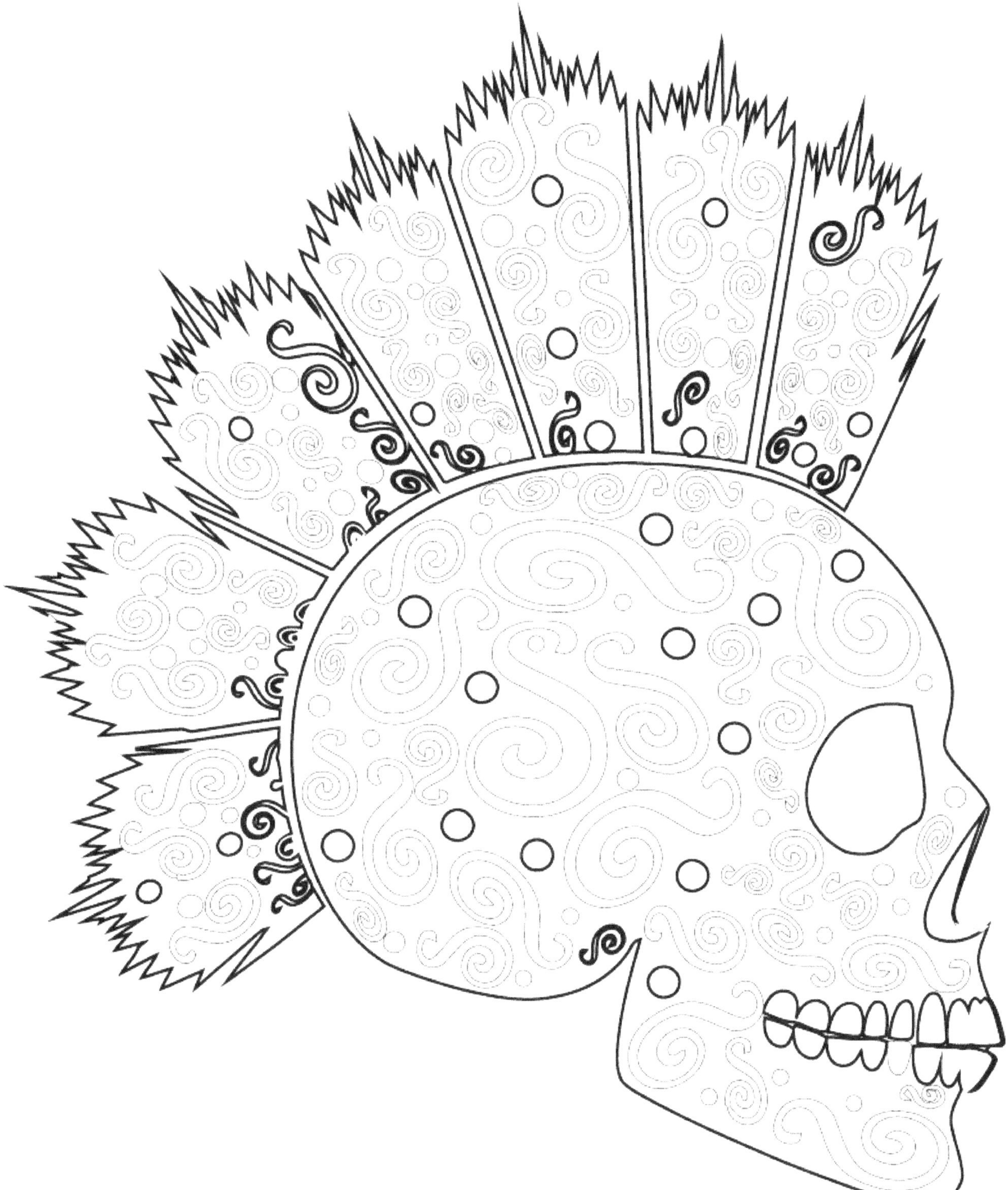

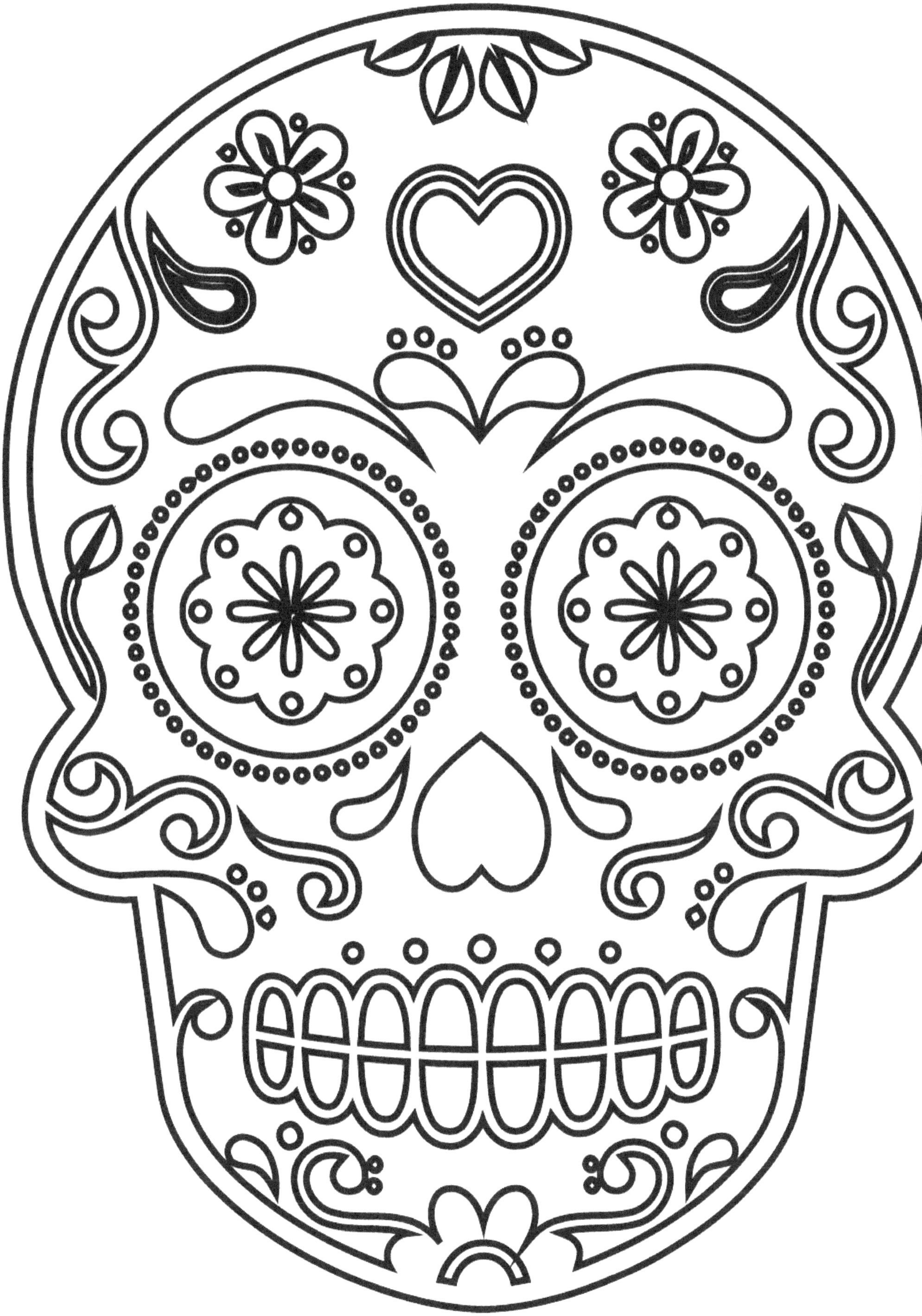

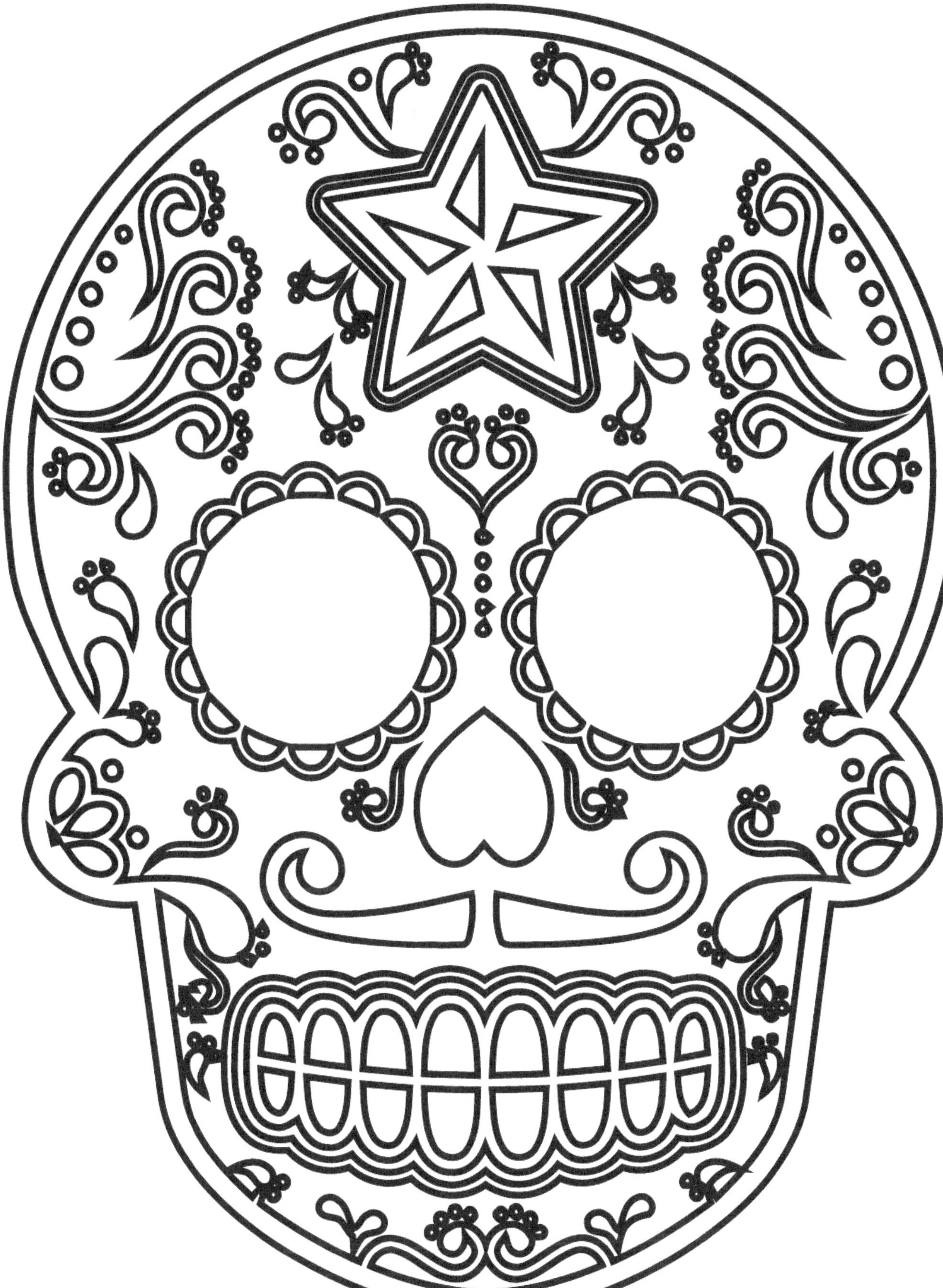

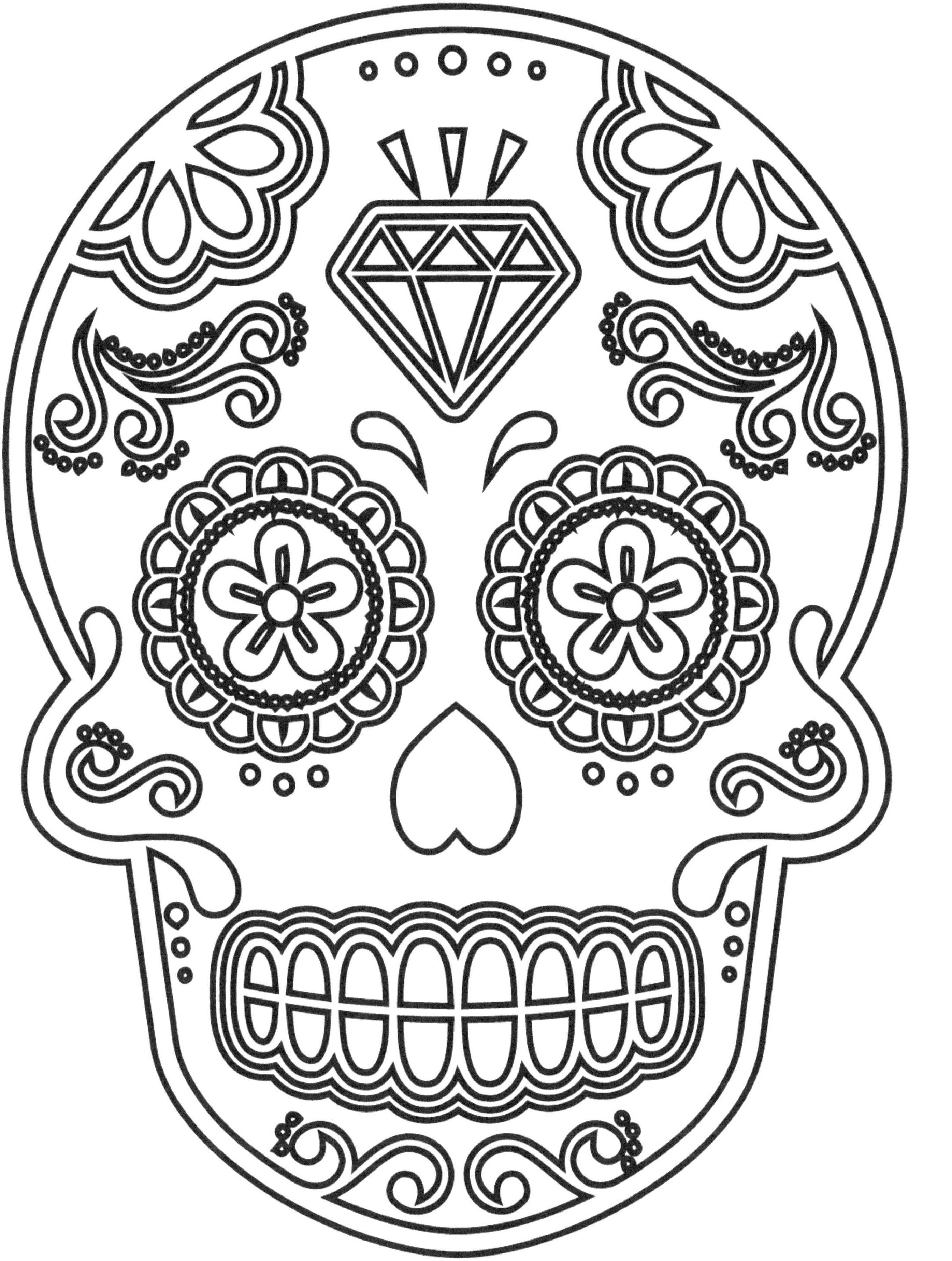

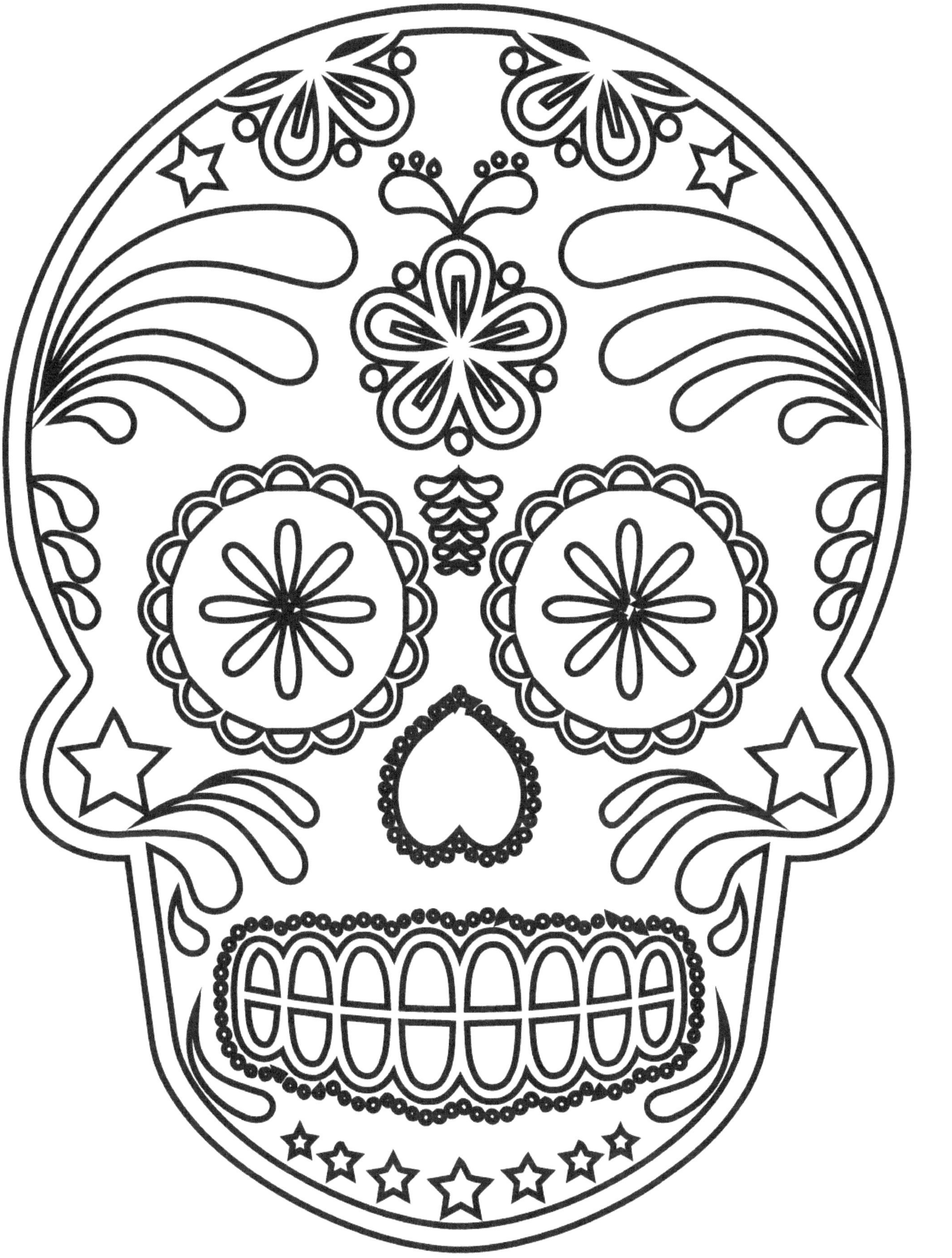

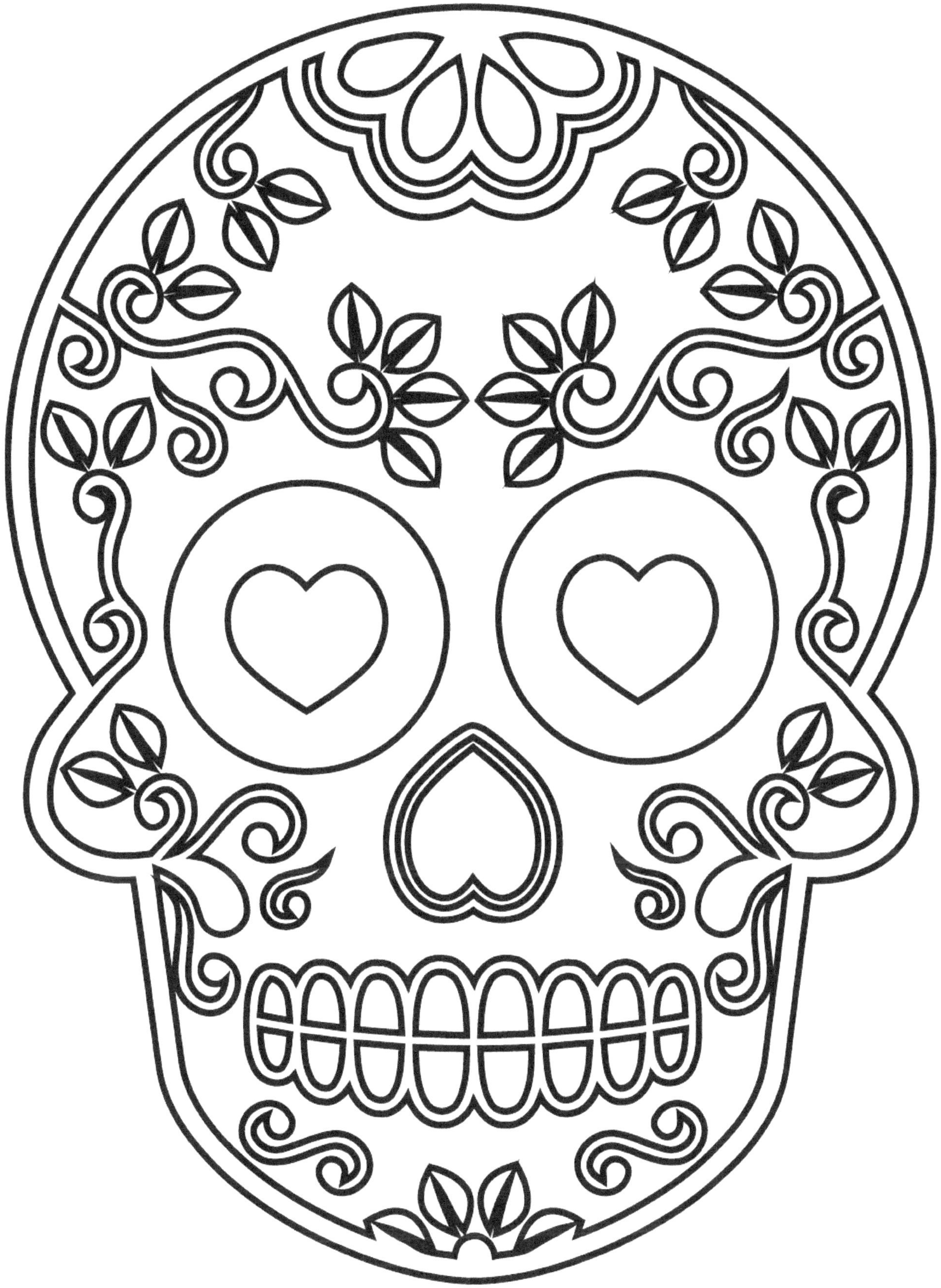

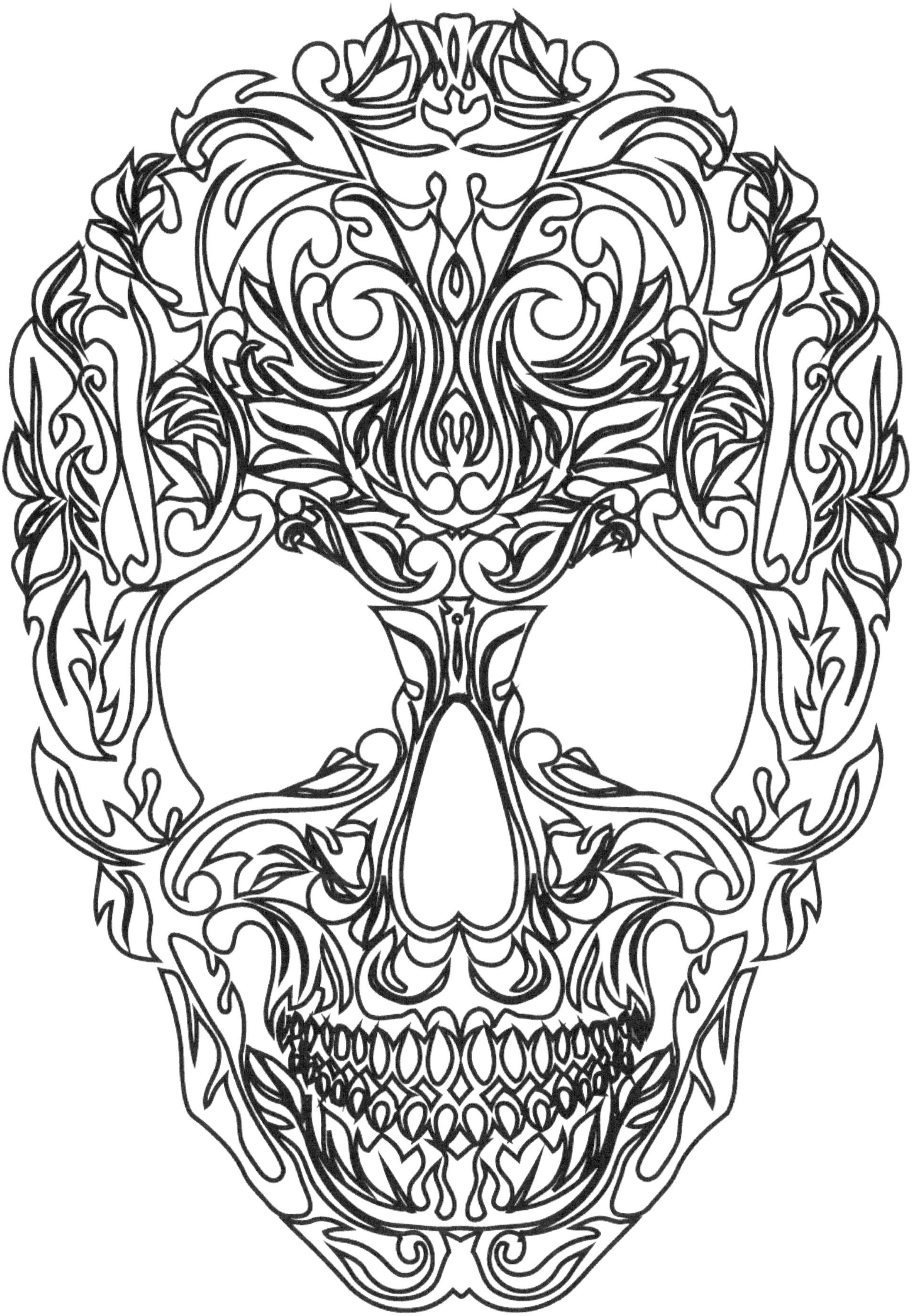

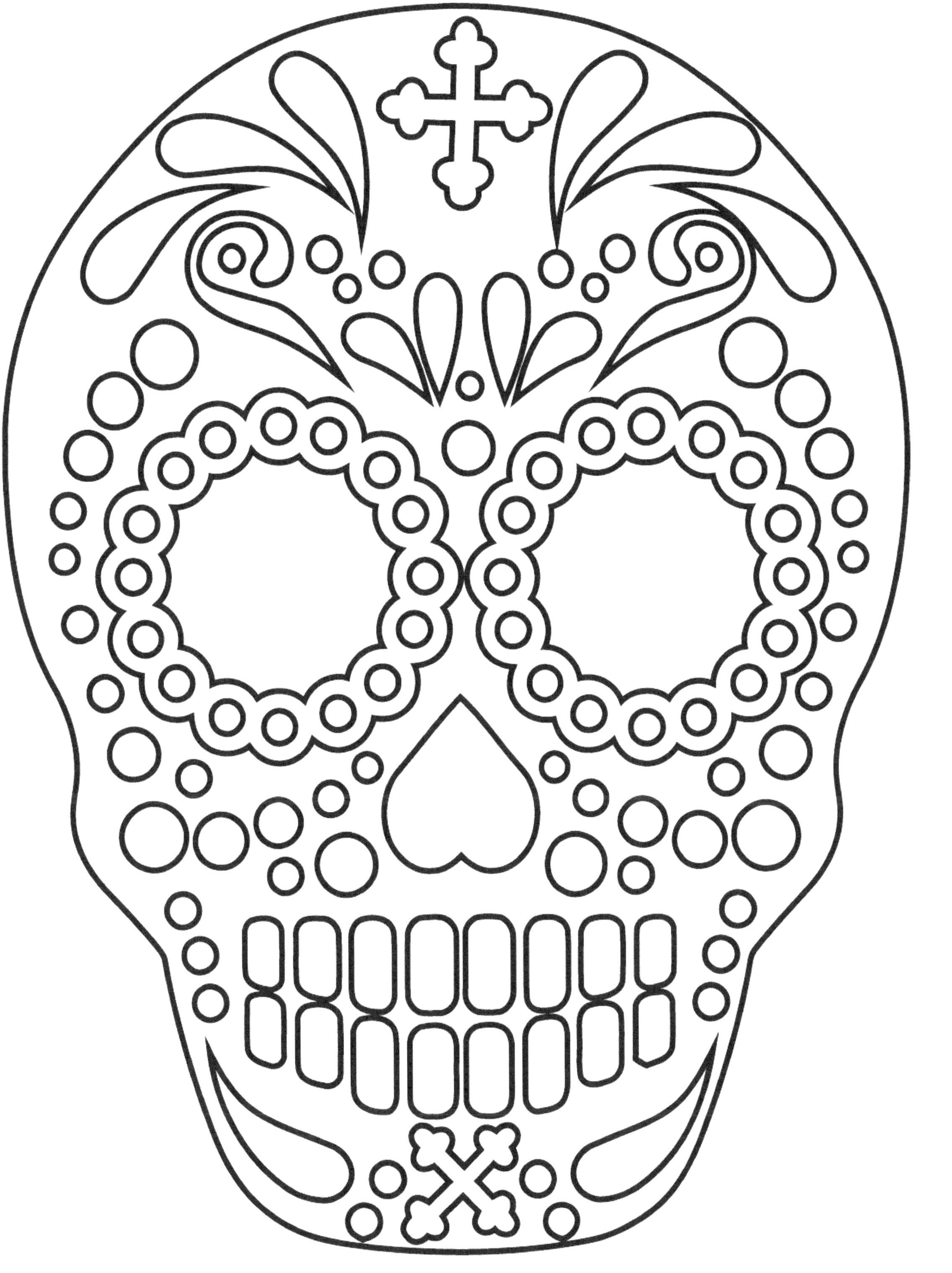

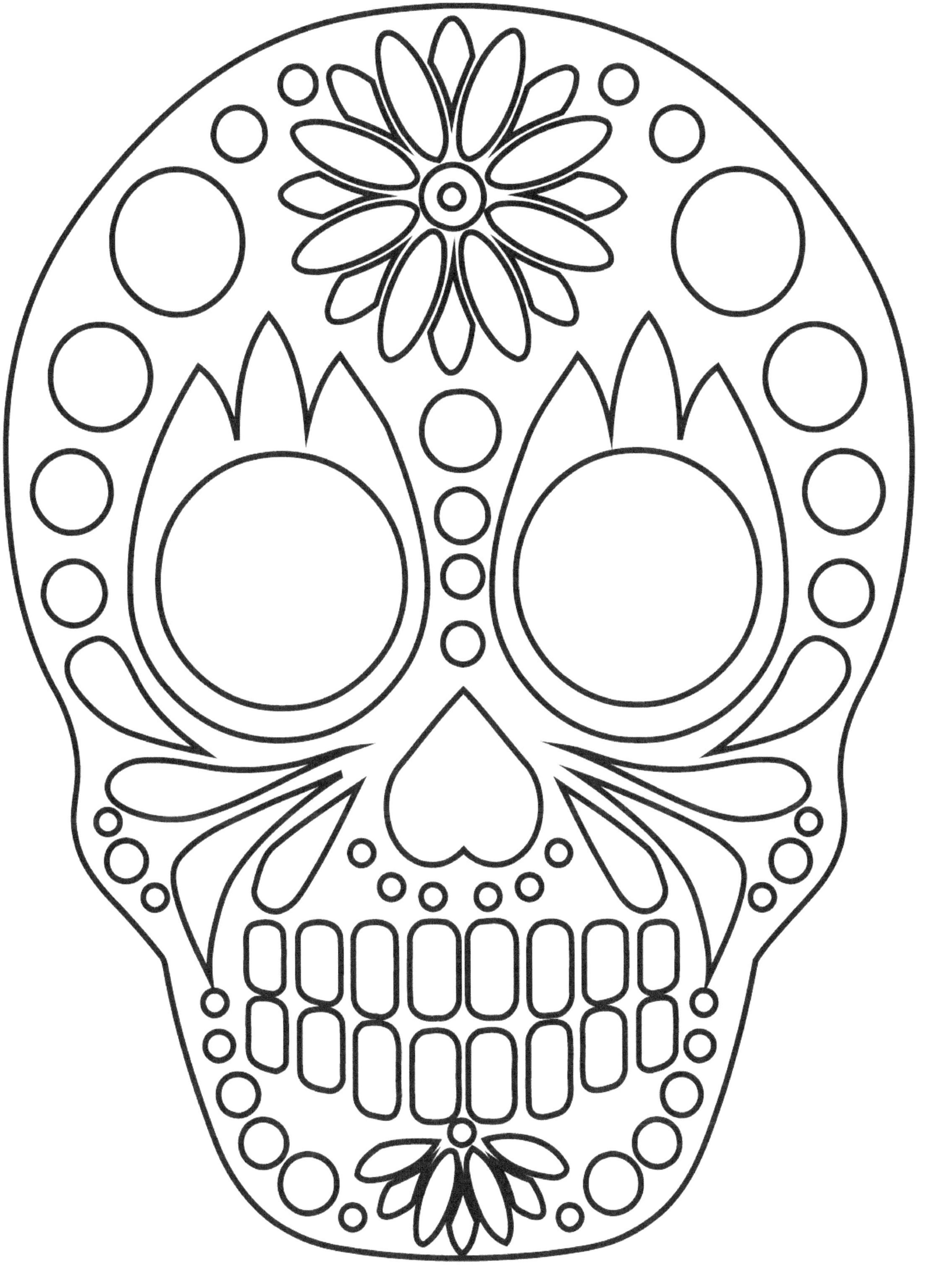

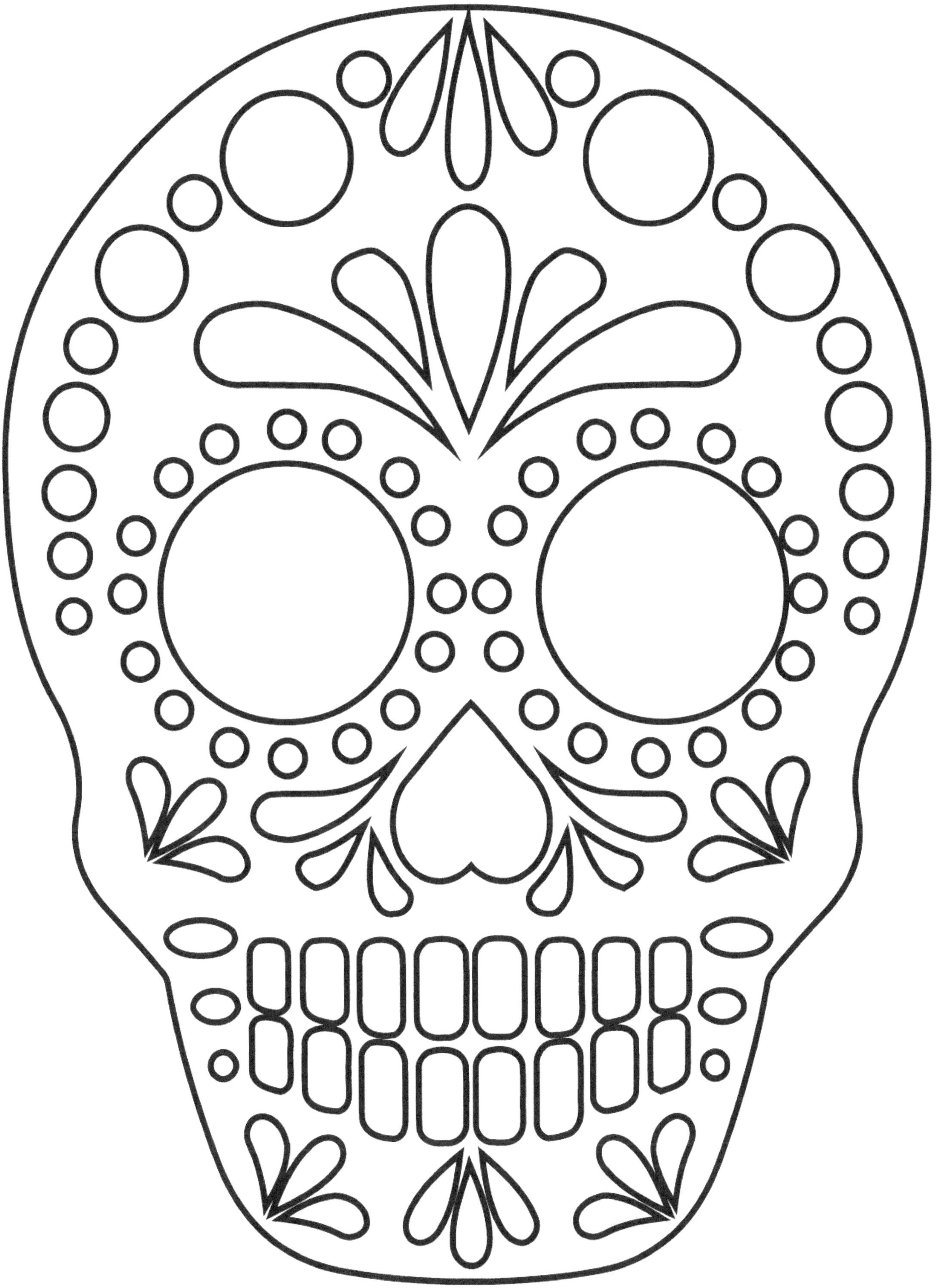

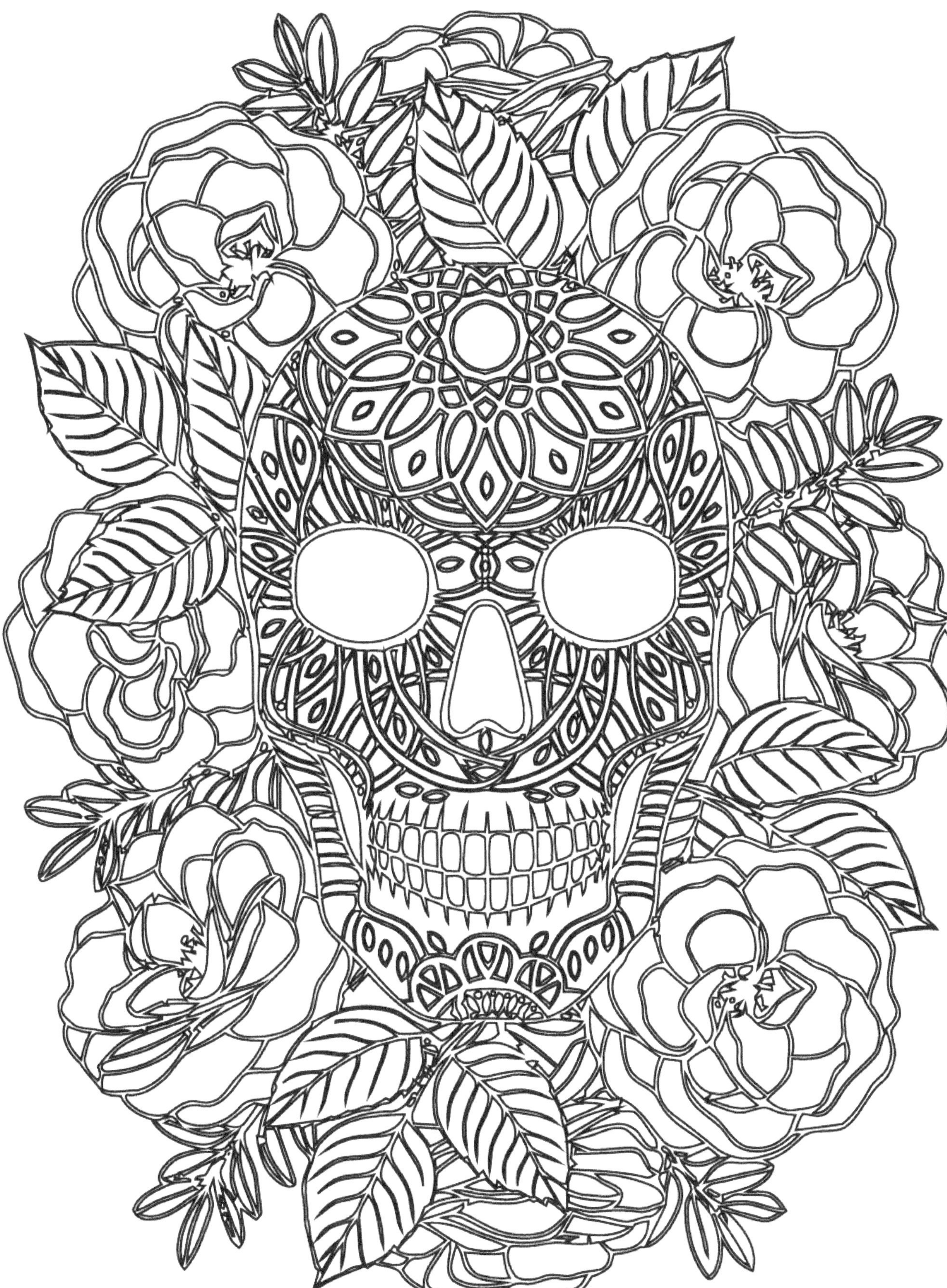

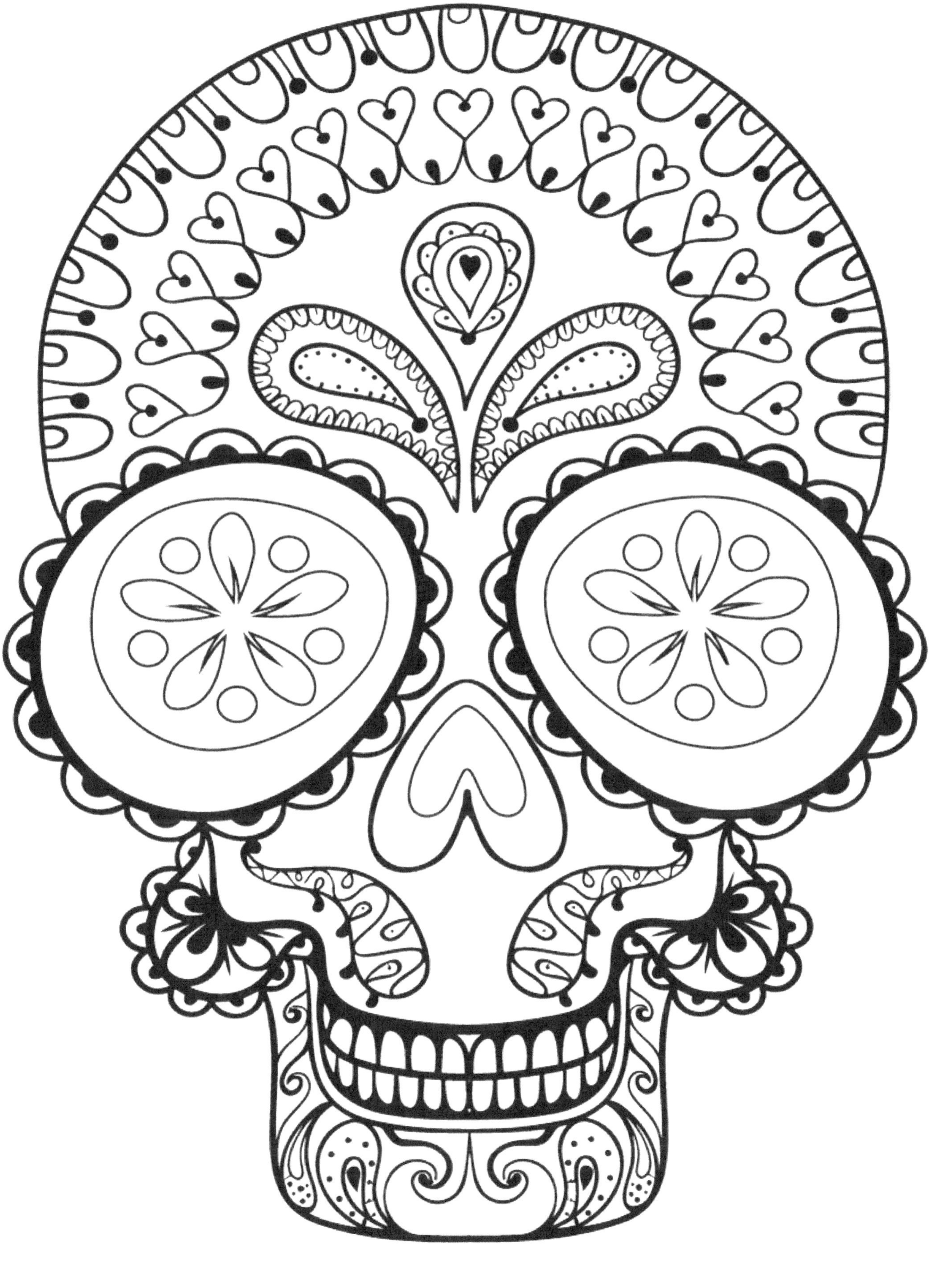

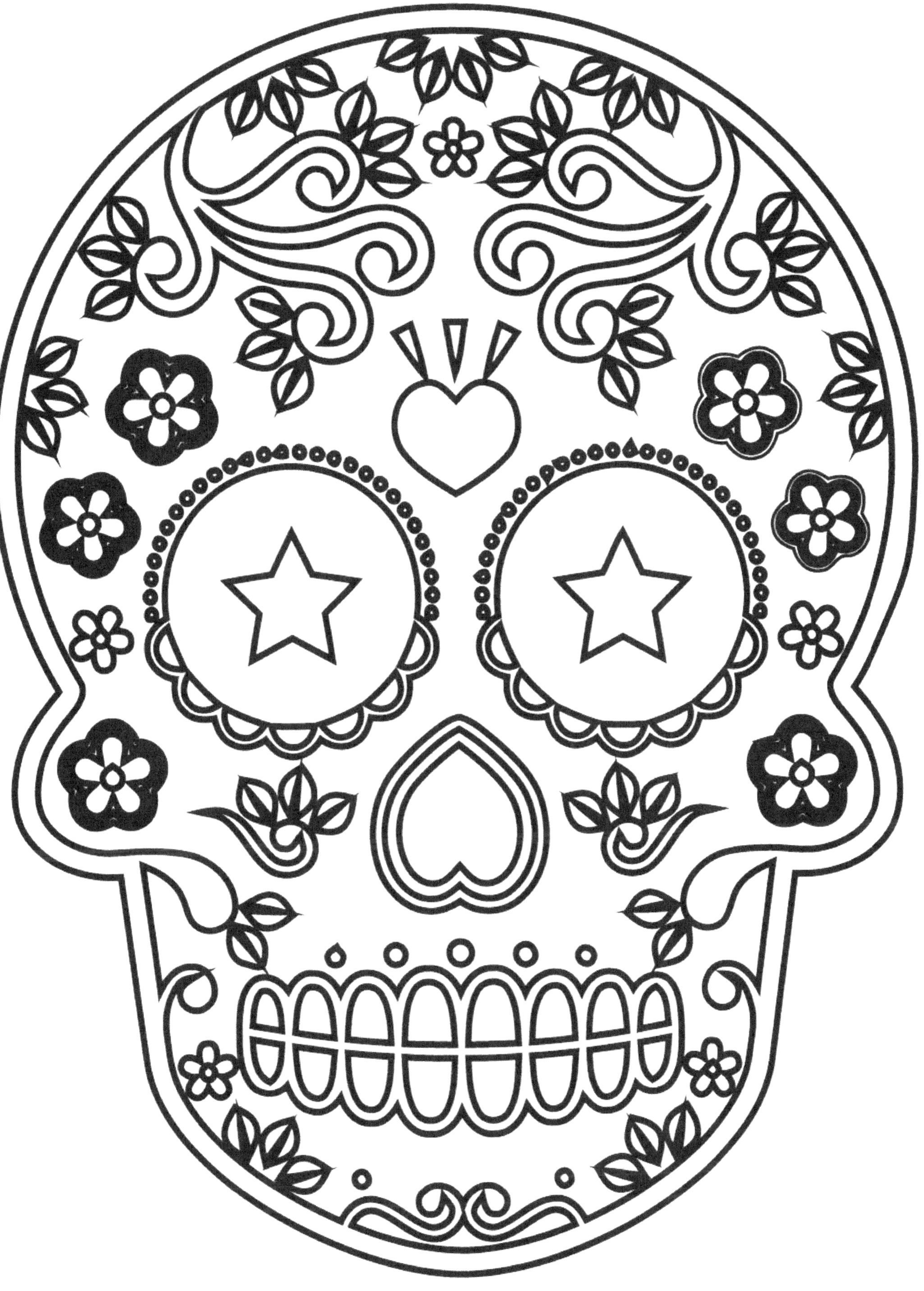

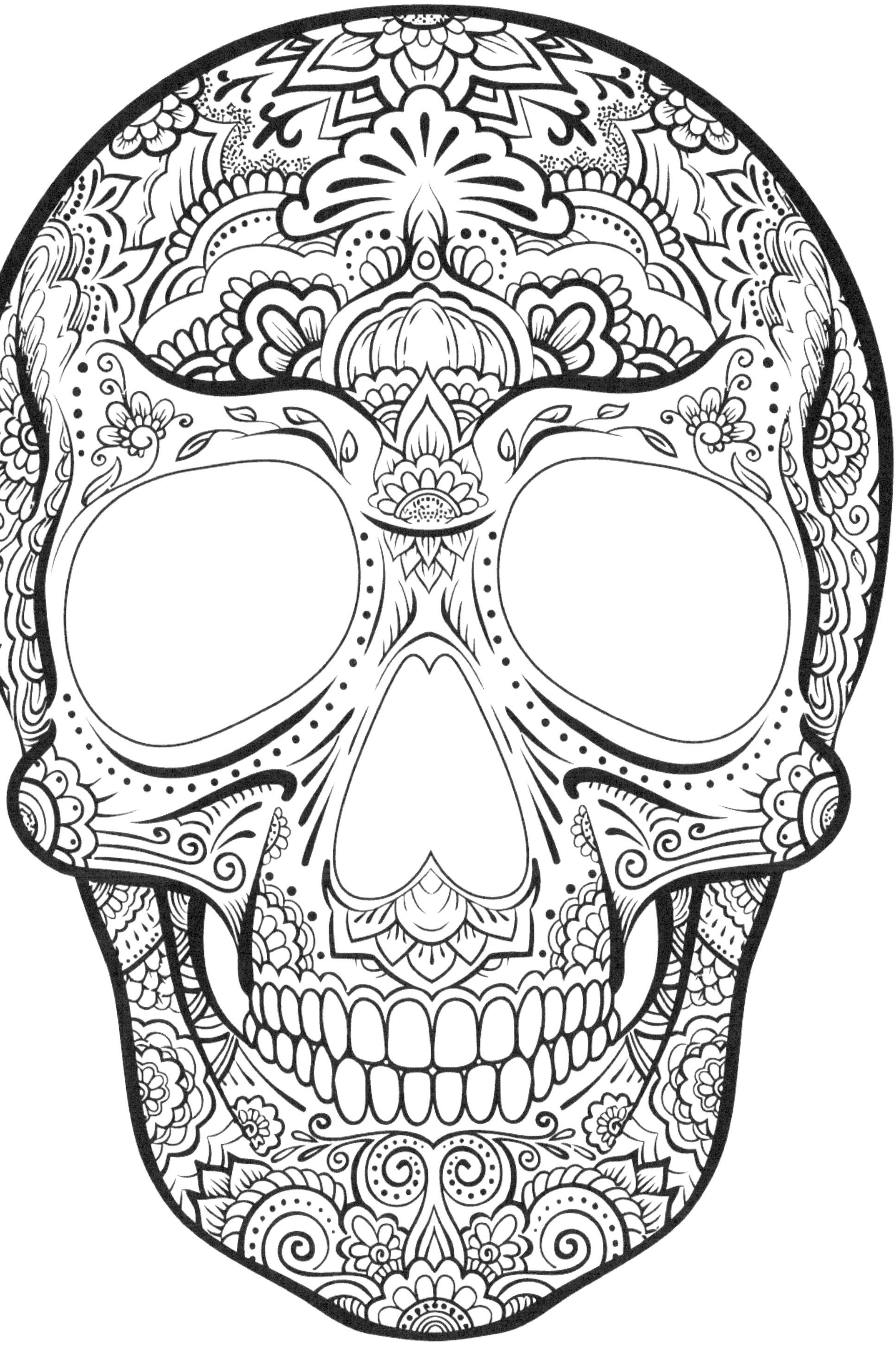

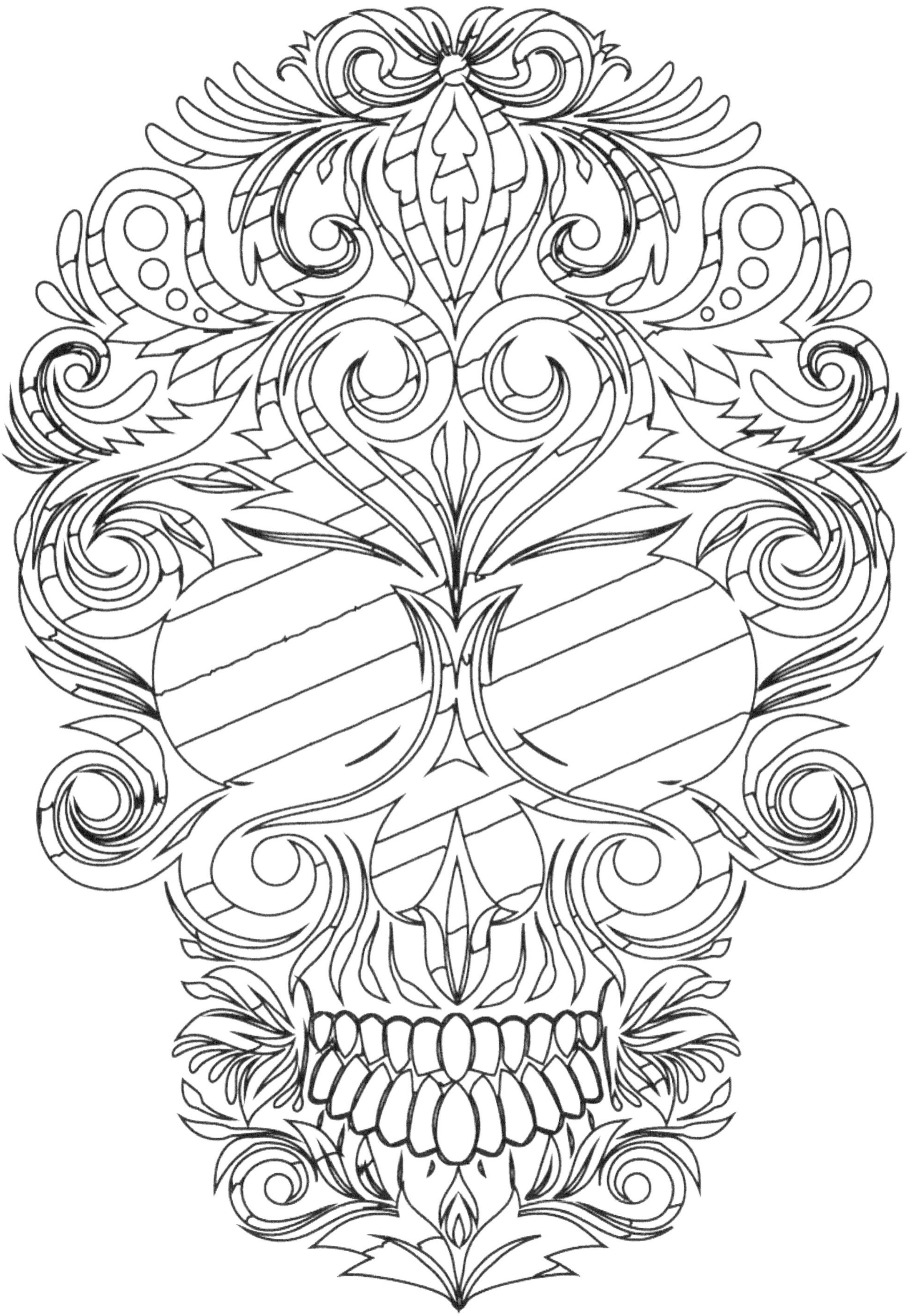

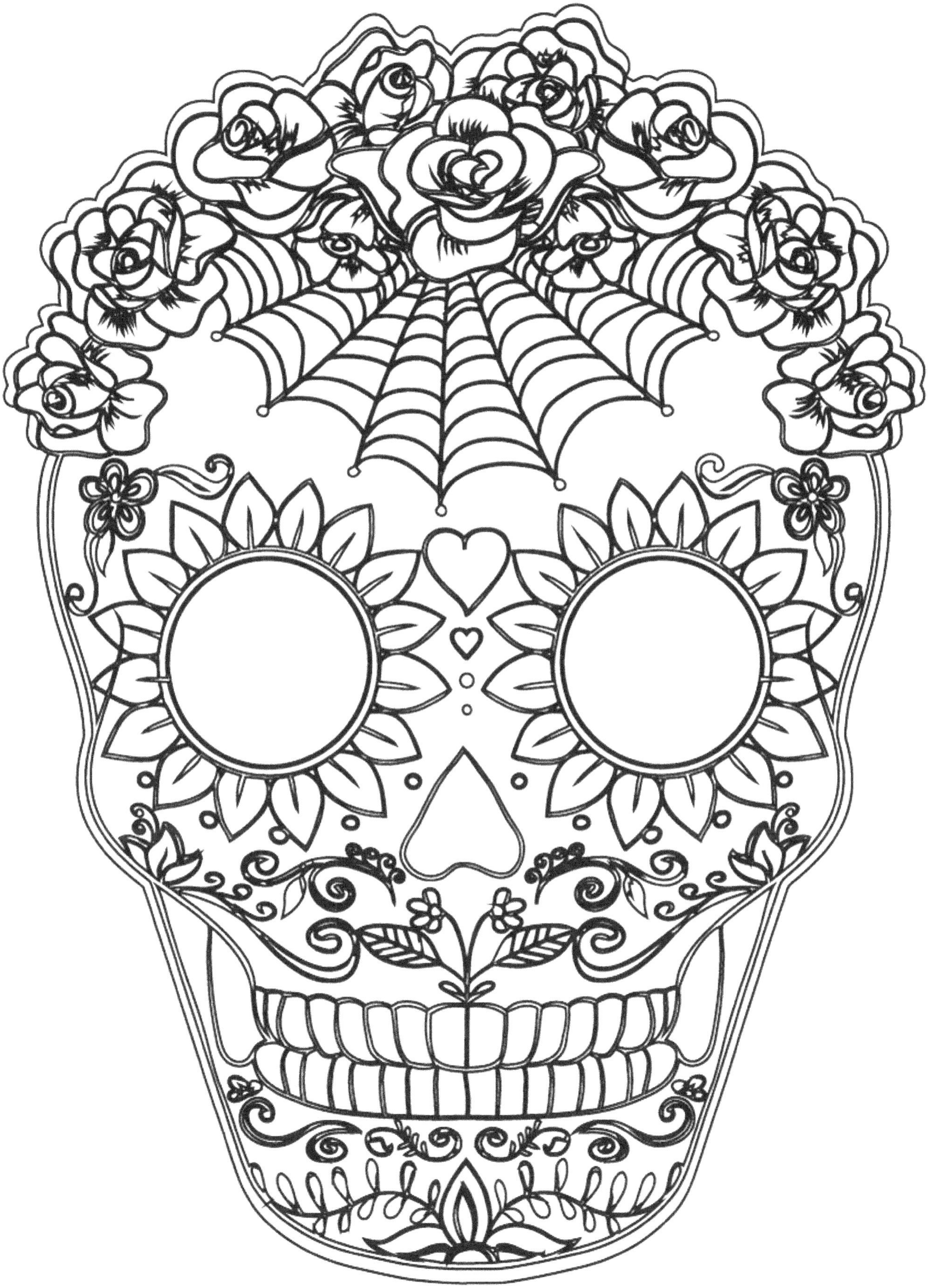

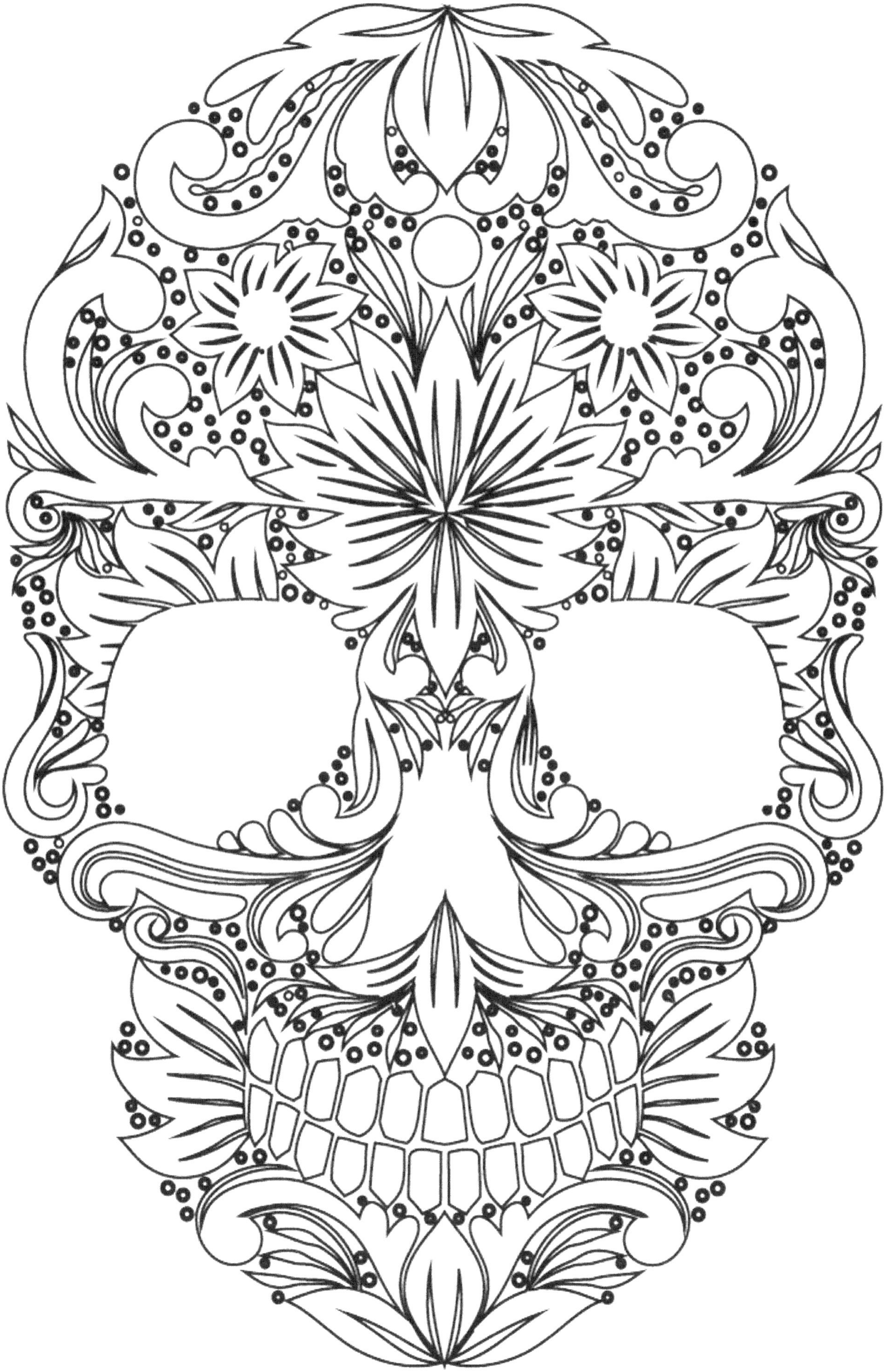